CAMBRIDGE LIBRARY COLLECTION

Books of enduring scholarly value

Travel and Exploration

The history of travel writing dates back to the Bible, Caesar, the Vikings and the Crusaders, and its many themes include war, trade, science and recreation. Explorers from Columbus to Cook charted lands not previously visited by Western travellers, and were followed by merchants, missionaries, and colonists, who wrote accounts of their experiences. The development of steam power in the nineteenth century provided opportunities for increasing numbers of 'ordinary' people to travel further, more economically, and more safely, and resulted in great enthusiasm for travel writing among the reading public. Works included in this series range from first-hand descriptions of previously unrecorded places, to literary accounts of the strange habits of foreigners, to examples of the burgeoning numbers of guidebooks produced to satisfy the needs of a new kind of traveller - the tourist.

Some Passages in the History of Eenoolooapik

Published in 1841, this is the story of Eenoolooapik, a young Inuit who guided whaling captain William Penny to the mouth of Cumberland Sound – a whale-rich body of water – 250 years after it was first explored and named by John Davis. Probably the first Inuk for whom a biography was published during his lifetime, 'Eenoo' drew a map which led Penny to the whaling area. His geographical knowledge therefore resulted in a burgeoning industry that provided seasonal employment to the Inuit and dramatically changed their lives. Alexander M'Donald (1817–48) describes Eenoolooapik's life and environment, a visit to Scotland with Penny (where he endeared himself to the people he met), and the difficulties he encountered in making the transition from life in the Arctic to nineteenth-century Britain. M'Donald himself later worked as an assistant surgeon on H.M.S. *Terror* in Sir John Franklin's last expedition: his eventual fate is not known.

T0349544

Cambridge University Press has long been a pioneer in the reissuing of out-of-print titles from its own backlist, producing digital reprints of books that are still sought after by scholars and students but could not be reprinted economically using traditional technology. The Cambridge Library Collection extends this activity to a wider range of books which are still of importance to researchers and professionals, either for the source material they contain, or as landmarks in the history of their academic discipline.

Drawing from the world-renowned collections in the Cambridge University Library, and guided by the advice of experts in each subject area, Cambridge University Press is using state-of-the-art scanning machines in its own Printing House to capture the content of each book selected for inclusion. The files are processed to give a consistently clear, crisp image, and the books finished to the high quality standard for which the Press is recognised around the world. The latest print-on-demand technology ensures that the books will remain available indefinitely, and that orders for single or multiple copies can quickly be supplied.

The Cambridge Library Collection will bring back to life books of enduring scholarly value (including out-of-copyright works originally issued by other publishers) across a wide range of disciplines in the humanities and social sciences and in science and technology.

Some Passages in the History of Eenoolooapik

A Young Esquimaux, Who Was
Brought to Britain in 1839

ALEXANDER M'DONALD

CAMBRIDGE
UNIVERSITY PRESS

CAMBRIDGE UNIVERSITY PRESS

Cambridge, New York, Melbourne, Madrid, Cape Town,
Singapore, São Paolo, Delhi, Tokyo, Mexico City

Published in the United States of America by Cambridge University Press, New York

www.cambridge.org
Information on this title: www.cambridge.org/9781108041058

© in this compilation Cambridge University Press 2012

This edition first published 1841
This digitally printed version 2012

ISBN 978-1-108-04105-8 Paperback

A NARRATIVE, &c.

EENOOLOOAPIK.

A NARRATIVE

OF SOME PASSAGES IN THE HISTORY OF

EENOOLOOAPIK,

A YOUNG ESQUIMAUX,

WHO WAS BROUGHT TO BRITAIN IN 1839, IN THE SHIP "NEPTUNE" OF ABERDEEN:

AN ACCOUNT OF THE

DISCOVERY OF HOGARTH'S SOUND:

REMARKS ON THE NORTHERN WHALE FISHERY,

AND SUGGESTIONS FOR ITS IMPROVEMENT, &c. &c.

BY ALEXANDER M'DONALD, L.R.C.S.E.

Member of the Cuverian Natural History Society of Edinburgh.

EDINBURGH: FRASER & CO.
AND J. HOGG, 116 NICOLSON STREET.
MDCCCXLI.

EDINBURGH: PRINTED BY J. HOGG, NICOLSON STREET.

PREFACE.

In presenting the following pages to the public, the Author may be allowed to offer a brief explanation of the reasons which led to their composition and publication. When, in the spring of 1840, he was engaged to accompany Captain Penny in the Bon Accord, in his professional capacity, it was suggested to him, in anticipation of the discovery of what has been denominated Hogarth's Sound, to prepare an account of the voyage, combined with some notices of the interesting Esquimaux whose information had first directed attention to that inlet as an eligible spot for the prosecution of the whale-fishery. Anticipating success in the discovery of a new field of enterprise, and judging that, besides the local interest attaching to the residence of Eenoolooapik in Aberdeen, there were circumstances connected with his visit to this country which rendered it of general, and even of national importance, the Author agreed to draw up, to the best of his ability, an account of the principal incidents of the voyage, in connection with what was known of the history of that intelligent and interesting individual.

Such is the *history* of the following " Narrative ;" and as it has been intended to be as comprehensive and explanatory of itself as possible, there is no need to enlarge upon the performance in a preface. The subject is one of considerable interest, and the Author has endeavoured to sustain that interest as far as practicable in the course of the Narrative. He has strictly adhered to truth in all the details, and he is not conscious of having misrepresented a single fact for the sake of effect.

There is one circumstance, however, in the Narrative, which he cannot allow to pass without notice. In proof of the progress which Eenoolooapik had made in writing, a fac simile of a letter which he wrote before he left the Bon Accord is inserted at page 102 ; and it might be inferred that it was meant to be affirmed that that letter was originated and executed entirely by Eenoolooapik himself. This is true so far, but not absolutely and altogether so. He had learned to know the

meaning of written language, and could
write many words both in English and
Esquimaux, but the letter which is given
in the following work was first written to
his dictation by the Author and then tran-
scribed by Eenoolooapik's own hand, and
without assistance, in the exact form in
which it is given in this volume. It will
be allowed that it is even thus a wonderful
proof of his intellectual capacity.

The Portrait which accompanies the work
is an excellent likeness of Eenoolooapik,
and may serve to shew to what extent
it is possible to improve the physical appearance of the Esquimaux. The Charts
are referred to in the places where they are
inserted, and they also explain themselves.
The Meteorological Tables at the end of
the volume will not interest general readers,
but they may be deemed of use in a scientific point of view.

In the hope that the subject treated of
is of sufficient importance to justify the
publication of this volume, it is given to
the world. There may be no merit in it
as a literary production, but let the vast
interests of which it treats be its recom-
mendation.

A NARRATIVE, &c.

CHAPTER I.

THE great want of success which has of late years attended the prosecution of the northern whale-fishery has led to its gradual diminution, and threatens soon to effect its total abandonment as a commercial pursuit. It is much to be regretted that a branch of commerce, by which a race of hardy and adventurous seamen may be trained to the perfection of maritime enterprise—our knowledge of the geography and natural history of the north extended —the wretched condition of the inhabitants of those dreary and sterile regions ameliorated, and the glad tidings of salvation conveyed to their shores,—should, in consequence of a few unfortunate seasons, be allowed to fall into utter neglect.

But common prudence and reason alike forbid the perseverance in an undertaking, which, for the most

B

part, hitherto, has proved so ruinous, unless some other and more effective method be devised for its continuance. An examination of the records of the fishery will shew, that, since 1834, a loss of life and property has been sustained sufficient to damp the ardour of the most adventurous and wealthy.

It is not difficult to account for these recent and repeated failures. The extensive accumulation of ice—resulting from the operation of causes not yet investigated or understood, but, in all probability, attributable to the revolution of a meteorological cycle, which the advanced science of some after age may evolve and elucidate—has rendered the navigation of those northern seas more difficult and dangerous, and the approach to the localities where the whales formerly abounded, generally impracticable till the season is far advanced. Another obvious cause exists in the animals having almost entirely deserted some of their usual haunts ; being forced, by the warfare which man wages against them, to seek shelter in the unexplored recesses of other and more peaceful seas.

To discover a fishery which combined the advantages of being productive and easily accessible, was a *desideratum* with the parties engaged in those toilsome and perilous enterprises. But the opinion seems generally to have been entertained, that the coasts of Davis' Strait had already been too minutely examined to admit of their disclosing any new field of adventure. The sequel will shew, however, that the conclusion was erroneous, and that there is at least one extensive inlet which had never been visited, where the whales are abundant and comparatively undisturbed.

In their intercourse with the natives at Durban, on the western coast, the fishermen had frequently been informed of the existence of a large inland sea, abounding with whales, and communicating with the Strait considerably to the southward of that locality. But the information thus obtained was altogether overlooked, until Captain Penny, commanding the Ship Neptune of Aberdeen, in 1839, directed his attention to the subject. Being satisfied that there was some truth in the statements of the natives regarding this matter, he brought home with him Eenoolooapik, a young Esquimaux of considerable intelligence, from whom, he had reason to think, much additional information might be obtained, not only on the subject of the whale-fishery, but also concerning the geography of those partially explored regions.

This interesting youth was a native of Keimooksook: a country stretching along the borders of that sea of which the Esquimaux had spoken. The history of his early years is a matter of uncertainty; but we may suppose, that beyond the simple inci-

dents of a savage boy's experience, who had been
nurtured amidst the cheerless solitudes of an arctic
clime and coast, there would be little to record or
commemorate, even although we possessed the necessary information. When he was about ten years
of age, his parents, impelled by curiosity, and ani-
mated by the hope of traffic, undertook a journey to
Durban, which they had learned from the neighbouring tribes, was a favourite place of resort with the
whalers. This journey of several hundred miles,
along a rugged and barren coast, exposed to all the
fury of the northern tempest, and often encumbered
with immense shoals of ice threatening hourly destruction to the daring navigator, these simple, but
hardy adventurers, accomplished in their frail *oomiak*
or luggage-boat ; and the necessity of keeping near
the shore afforded Eenoolooapik an ample opportunity of acquiring that knowledge of the coast which
afterwards proved of such signal importance to him.

Arrived at Durban, they settled among the inhabitants ; and it may be inferred from some passages
in their private history, communicated by Eenoo (as
we shall now and then familiarly call him), that they
afterwards rose to considerable importance. The
circumstance which attested the aggrandizement of
the family, was nothing less than the fact of Eenoo's
father assuming the patriarchal prerogative of espous-
ing another of the fair daughters of the land, in

consideration of the fading beauty of Nootaapik—a matron whom we shall afterwards have occasion to notice in the course of our narrative as the mother of Eenoolooapik.

The proximity of Durban harbour to the residence of the Esquimaux, afforded Eenoolooapik frequent opportunities of visiting the ships; and it may well be supposed, that the equipment of the vessels, and the superiority of all their arrangements, would fill the inexperienced mind of the savage with sublime conceptions of the intelligence of the *Kudloonite.** Every day of his intercourse with the fishermen added to the strength of this feeling; and so powerful did it at last become, that he resolved, should ever an opportunity occur, upon visiting *the land of the white men.*†

On several occasions, both in 1837 and 1838, he attempted to carry this resolution into effect, but the tears and entreaties of his mother prevailed, and diverted him from his purpose till the opportunities were past. However, he continued to cherish the determination of making a voyage to *Kudloonite noona,* and at last an unexpected circumstance afforded him the means of gratifying his wishes. While Captain Penny was, in 1839, engaged in

---

* That is, the white men.

† In Esquimaux, *Kudloonite noona.*

making inquiries among the Esquimaux at Durban, regarding the situation of the inland sea already referred to, and its eligibility for the purposes of the whale-fishery, he had occasion to examine Eenooloo-apik on the subject; and finding him familiar with the features of the country, he requested him to trace an outline of the coast. This, after he was made to comprehend the method and object of it, he perform-ed with remarkable facility. He delineated a chart in which he represented the shore as abruptly leav-ing the general coast-line of Davis' Strait, and stretching to the westward for about sixty miles; then trending to the northward until it arrived at a point which he described as being immediately opposite to Durban. From this point a deep inlet, named by the Esquimaux Kingaïte, penetrated so far into the land, in the direction of Durban, as almost to insulate the portion to the southward. From the entrance to this inlet, the shore again took a westerly direction for about forty miles, when another deep inlet, named Kingoua, formed the termination of the sea to the northward. The shore was then laid down as returning to the southward, in a direction almost parallel to that already deli-neated. The eastern coast was represented as being bold and precipitous, intersected by numerous bays and creeks, and a few clusters of islands scattered along it. The western shore was stated to be low,

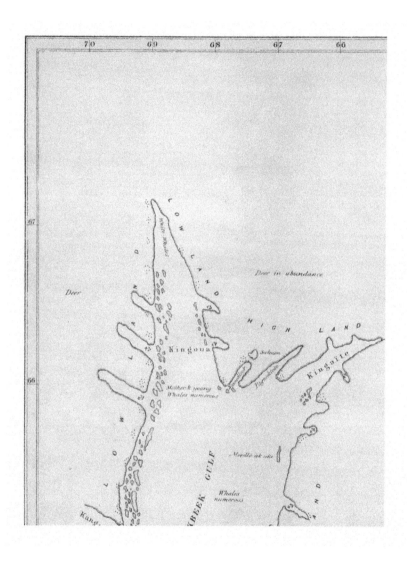

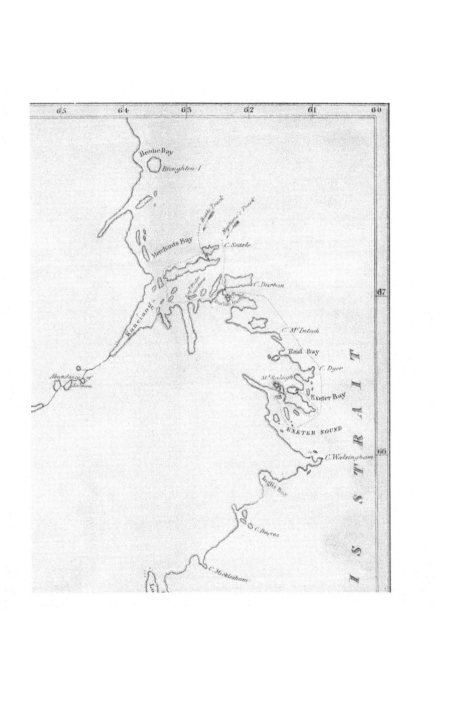

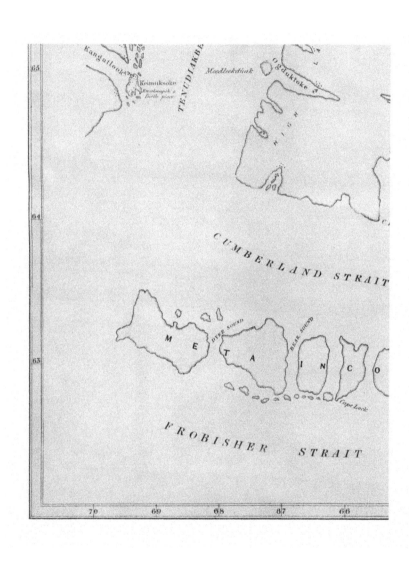

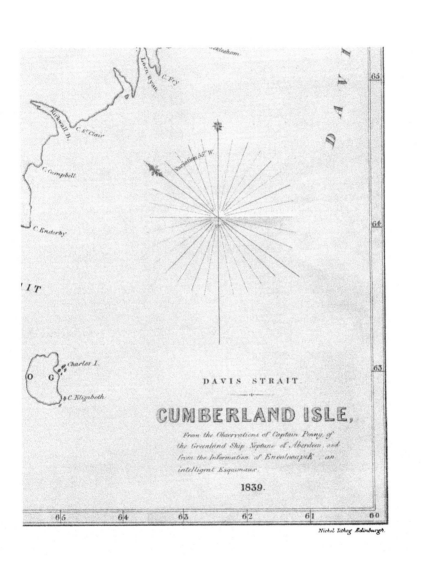

DAVIS STRAIT.

CUMBERLAND ISLE,

From the Observations of Captain Penny, of the Greenland Ship Neptune of Aberdeen, and from the Information of Enealooapik, an intelligent Esquimaux.

1839.

Nichol Lithog. Edinburgh.

and almost concealed in its whole extent by a dense
mass of islands. He described the coast as being
inhabited by numerous tribes of Esquimaux, and
stated that they were in the practice of killing considerable numbers of whales for the sake of their
flesh, which there forms a staple article of food. The
general name which he gave to the sea thus laid
down, was *Tenudiackbeek*,—a name supposed to have
some reference to the number of whales frequenting
it.* This supposition is rendered the more probable
from the circumstance of the names assigned by him
to various other localities, being generally expressive
of something for which they were remarkable.

The knowledge he displayed in the execution of
this sketch † induced Captain Penny to invite him

---

* The word *ackbuk* signifies, in the language of the Esquimaux of the west land, a whale ; and in the plural it is *ackbeek*
or *ackbeelik :* but the writer was unable, from all his inquiries
at Eenoolooapik, to trace the etymology of the word *Tenudiackbeek* farther.

† We beg to present our readers with a copy of Enoolooa-
pik's performance, as reduced from the Chart published at
the Hydrographic Office of the Admiralty, after the original
sketch executed by Eenoo in 1839. It will be remarked, that
Tenudiackbeek is made to enter from Cumberland Strait, but
upon examination this was found to be incorrect. This, however, was no error of Eenoolooapik's : and the reason for as-
signing that particular feature to the Chart will be given in

to Britain. An invitation so much in accordance
with his own resolution was at once, and without
hesitation, accepted ; and his relations were immediately apprised of his determination.

October had now arrived, when all, save the rude
denizens of the north, must leave those bleak, ice-
bound shores ; and Eenoo having obtained the consent of his friends, was taken on board the Neptune,
accompanied by a number of his tribe. The Esquimaux, with the exception of his mother, shewed
little emotion at parting with him. With her, however, the case was far otherwise. Her first-born—
now the chief guardian and support of her declining
years—was about to visit a country and a clime far
distant and unknown ; to sojourn among a people
whose language and manners he knew not ;—and the
promise of a stranger was her only guarantee for his
safety. Under such circumstances it was not to be
wondered at that maternal affection, implanted alike
in the breast of the civilized and savage, should be

---

an after part of the narrative. By comparing Eenoolooapik's
delineation with the Chart of Captain Penny's discoveries, in
a subsequent part of this work, it will be seen that, upon
the whole, with the exception just noticed, the difference is
but trifling ; and that it exhibits in a striking degree the
aptitude of Eenoolooapik's mind for geographical knowledge
and observation.

displayed in all its power. Untrammelled by formal and frigid restraint, which oft-times checks the pure feelings of nature, and freezes the gushings-forth of the holiest affections, this unsophisticated Esquimaux gave vent to her emotions in loud and prolonged bursts of wailing and tears. These expressions of her feelings lasted for some time, assuming various and somewhat extravagant phases, until, at last, in accordance with the peculiar manners of her country on such occasions, she laid bare her bosom, and invited him by an appeal, which, though silent, was irresistible, to kiss the warm breast which in infancy had suckled him: such being the last tender testimony of affection when the grave may prevent another meeting upon earth. At this touching scene Eenoo's resolution had well-nigh deserted him; but in a moment he rallied: the settled purpose of his soul was not now to be so easily subdued.

At this time Eenoolooapik was about twenty years of age, and might be considered, in his physical aspect, a fair specimen of the Esquimaux race. But, as yet, his mental acquirements were of a very limited description. Doomed hitherto to pass his days amid those dismal solitudes of snow, where all his energies were requisite to provide for the wants of the passing hour, and where mental cultivation is unknown, it was scarcely to be expected that he would manifest much knowledge beyond what he had gathered in his wanderings, or what had been forced upon him by daily experience. And, indeed, if we except his geographical information, there was little to recommend him to the notice of our countrymen; but *that* being observed to be considerable, it was deemed of importance to have a better opportunity of learning the extent of it, as it might not only be made available for the purposes of the whale-fishery, but also be of value in a scientific point of view. Hence, as before observed, the reason of his invitation to Britain.

During the homeward passage every care was taken to instruct him in the usages of civilized society; and aided by the faculty of imitation, which he possessed in a very high degree, he adopted the manners of those around him with astonishing facility. Every attention was bestowed to prevent his morals being contaminated by intercourse with the vicious; and this was the more necessary, as the first impressions made upon a mind emerging from the gloom of savage ignorance, were likely to be permanent. His docility and the mildness of his disposition soon rendered him a general favourite; and the kindness which he in consequence experienced, no doubt contributed largely to the favourable opinion which he formed regarding the *Kudloonite.* At first he was rather averse to the change of dress which it was necessary he should adopt; for though it might please the eye and gratify his passion for embellishment, it was yet felt exceedingly inconvenient and irksome, and he would gladly have exchanged it for the loose furs to which he had been accustomed. He soon acquired habits of extreme personal cleanliness,—a circumstance the more surprising, that the Esquimaux are generally very inattentive in that respect; but so complete was the revolution which his ideas underwent on this point of propriety, that in a short time he shewed an inclination to be rather fastidious than negligent.

An ample opportunity was now afforded Captain Penny for examining Eenoolooapik more minutely concerning Tenudiackbeek; and a kind of conventional language, composed of an intermixture of English and Esquimaux, being established between them, Eenoo communicated many further particulars on that and other subjects; and when language altogether failed him, he readily supplied its place by a rude drawing. In this manner, too, he represented his countrymen as engaged in encountering the various dangers of the chase, and thus conveyed to the mind a much more accurate idea than could possibly have been done by his imperfect verbal expression.

The description which he had given concerning the entrance to Tenudiackbeek, and the charts of the most recent discoverers shewing no inlet of any extent between Durban and Cape Enderby, led

Captain Penny at once to suppose that it communicated with the sea by means of Cumberland Strait. The direction, too, which the coast at the entrance was represented as taking, and the knowledge that that Strait is to this time but imperfectly explored, both combined to favour that opinion.

In going over the chart, Eenoo would not only describe the particular features of each place, but point out the situations remarkable for the occurrence of some tragical event. While engaged in this manner, he related the circumstance of a shipwreck, which was listened to with the deepest attention. He stated that the Esquimaux had informed him, that nearly four years before, when the sun was very low, they had seen a ship wrecked among the ice off the west land, to the southward of Durban,— supposed, from his description, to have been about the place called Saunderson's Tower. They had told him that the crew pitched their tents upon the ice, and remained there for several days, when, seeing another ship in the offing, they, leaving ten of their number dead upon the ice, set out in the hope of reaching her. The period and place of this occurrence, the season of the year, *when the sun was very low,*—supposed to have been about the month of February,—all conspired to point it out as the loss of the ship William Torr of Hull. That vessel, it will be remembered, was beset among the ice during the winter of 1835-6,

and never afterwards heard of. Her unfortunate
crew had doubtless perished in the attempt to reach
the ship which they had seen;—and, except this
brief and uncertain intelligence, no memorial of their
sad destiny remains, to tell to their sorrowing relations and friends of the dreadful misery and death
which were their portion.

For the purpose of recording the duration of his
absence from home, Eenoolooapik had recourse to the
expedient of casting a knot upon a cord every morning when he arose; and when any unusual event
happened, he cast a double knot to mark the period
of its occurrence. On making the land, a double
knot was cast; but his attention then became so much
absorbed by the variety of extraordinary objects
which were every hour presented to him, that the
cord was laid aside and neglected. The frequent
repetition of the words, Kudloonite! Kudloonite!
(the white men! the white men!), pronounced in
a slow, drawling manner, which he always assumed
when much pleased with any thing, was the only
expression of admiration which escaped him. When
proceeding close along the land, he remarked the
distance of the houses from the water; a circumstance which surprised him so much, that he expressed great astonishment that people could live in such
situations. He seemed, as yet, to have had no idea
of the possibility of deriving the means of subsistence

from any other source than the sea. Nor is it wonderful that he should have held this opinion, for his experience had been gathered from his own barren land, which produces little fitted for the purposes of man, save the moss for his winter's lamp.

He was first taken on shore on the coast of Caithness, at a place called the Castle of Mey. He expressed himself highly delighted with the sight of the Castle, and wished much to obtain a view of the interior of the building. This, however, was denied him by the keeper of the mansion, who, with true Cerberus-like obstinacy, refused to allow the party even to walk round it.

A circumstance occurred here, which, while it afforded considerable amusement to those about him, manifested the extreme simplicity of his ideas regarding the variety and extent of the animal creation. On seeing a cow and pony quietly grazing together, he stooped down and made towards them with the utmost caution, acting as he had been accustomed to do in the chase. When sufficiently near, he signified by a motion of his arm that they offered an excellent mark for an arrow. Observing the mirth of his companions, he returned and asked what kind of *deer* they were? or whether they were not *all the same as the Esquimaux dogs?* Hitherto he had been ignorant of the existence of animals diverse from those with which he had been familiar; but being now undeceived, and at a loss for any other name by which to distinguish them, his mind reverted to those denizens of his own country as the only prototypes of the quadrupeds now before him. In the same way, when he first tasted a piece of cod-fish, he declared it was excellent *salmon*, or "all the same," as he expressed it; meaning, simply, that it was a fish bearing some resemblance to the salmon, with which he was well acquainted.

The Neptune had now arrived off Aberdeen, but the wind blowing from the eastward, a heavy sea ran upon the bar, and prevented her from taking the harbour. After contending for several days against an increasing gale, she was run up the Frith of Forth, and anchored under the island of Inchkeith. Here the Sovereign, steam-ship, of Aberdeen, was also lying, and Eenoo was taken on board that vessel. One of the passengers, not calculating upon Eenoo's keen sense of truth and right, and wishing to afford himself and others some amusement at the expense of the untutored Esquimaux, took from his neck his gold watch-chain and threw it around that of Eenoo, who, somewhat surprised at the munificence of the stranger, asked if he meant to bestow it upon him. Being assured of this, he walked away, taking no further notice of the matter, till the gentleman becoming concerned for the safety of his property, began to insist for its return. To this, however,

Eenoo objected ; saying, " you give me to take from
me—not good—*Innuit* (the Esquimaux) no do that:"
—thus reading the gentleman a lecture in moral
philosophy which he was not prepared to expect from
such a quarter. Eenoo's firm refusal to deliver up
the prize caused considerable merriment among the
rest of the passengers, and he persisted in retaining
it until the interposition of Captain Penny procured
its immediate restoration.

This jest was no doubt attempted without the
slightest intention of corrupting Eenoo, but it was
obviously calculated to make a bad impression upon
his inexperienced mind, as it tended to destroy those
principles of rectitude which the Esquimaux act
upon among themselves. They are blamed, and not
without reason, for being dishonest in their intercourse with us, and it is highly probable that this
propensity was at first called into activity by trifling
circumstances such as that now detailed. It requires
little philosophy to account for this: for, finding
deceit and falsehood practised towards themselves,
and at the same time having strong temptations
placed before them in the shape of articles useful to
them, and unattainable from any other source, it is
noways strange that they yield themselves up to the
practice of secret cunning and appropriation.

Among the multiplicity of objects which Eenoolooapik saw in sailing along the coast, the light-

houses seemed to interest him the most; and of
these the erection on the Bell-Rock attracted the
greatest share of his attention. Concerning this
structure, he asked whether it was one stone or rock?
and whether it had not been brought from the land
and placed where he saw it? He was easily informed
of the mode of its erection and its use; and, indeed,
the aptitude which he displayed in comprehending
the nature of the many objects brought under his
notice, was a matter of astonishment to all around
him.

The weather having now moderated, they left the
Frith and pursued their way back to Aberdeen,
where they arrived on the night of the 8th November.
Gaining the harbour while it was dark, there
was no opportunity of witnessing how Eenoo would
have expressed himself on a sudden view of the city
bursting upon him. The novelties which every day
since his arrival on the coast had revealed, had in
some measure prepared his mind for what he was
about to witness; but there can be no doubt that
his anticipations of society and scenery had fallen
far short of that to which he was afterwards introduced. His residence in this country forming a
distinct era in his history, we shall not enter upon
that matter in the present chapter, but shall devote
the next division of our narrative to a review of the
incidents of that eventful period, interspersing it

D

with such reflections as occur to us in passing, or which seem to arise naturally from the subject under consideration.

CHAPTER II.

THERE is a feeling of romantic interest associated in the minds of most people with the arrival of " strangers and foreigners" on our shores ; and this principle of curiosity, as it is sometimes called, is heightened if the visitants be of a rude, uncivilized race. If it is not the same, it seems to be akin to the motive which induces us to visit a menagerie or a museum ; although, when we gaze upon a fellow mortal in the uncouth aspect of barbarism, there may be more of *sympathy* mingled with the feeling than when we study the habits and instincts of the natural denizens of the forest. Mind is a subject of wonderful contemplation, whether exhibited in the refinement and science of civilized life, or in the wild, uncultivated manners of savage existence ; and when a real " son of the desert" is brought amongst us, we naturally feel a strong desire to witness the workings of his untutored reason, and the develop- ment and display of energies which have slumbered till the moment he is ushered into the midst of civilization.

The news of the arrival of an Esquimaux in Aberdeen produced considerable sensation among all classes of the inhabitants; and on the following day great numbers of people collected on the quay for the purpose of obtaining a sight of Eenoolooapik. The cabin of the Neptune, too, was crowded with visitors, and Eenoo was thus subjected to much that was disagreeable and foreign to his constitution, in the confinement and increasing heat of the narrow accommodation. He was, in consequence of being thus exposed to an overheated and vitiated atmosphere, seized with a pulmonary affection, which, though slight at first, the humidity and somewhat variable nature of our climate tended to aggravate. It will shortly be our painful duty to record a period of protracted and severe suffering which he endured, and which, but for the very assiduous and efficient treatment of his medical attendant, Dr Pirrie, and the fatherly attention of Captain Penny and other kind friends, might have terminated fatally; but the melancholy task is spared us for some time, till we trace a brief account of his introduction to refined society, and the effect which it had upon his ready and retentive mind.

He was now transferred from the Neptune to the more comfortable accommodation of a town residence; and the same facility of comprehension was displayed by him in reference to every thing to which he was introduced. Shortly after his arrival he was invited to a dinner party, given expressly for the purpose of ascertaining how he would conduct himself amongst the higher and more fashionable circles of society, before an opportunity had been afforded him of becoming acquainted with the forms which are there observed. On this occasion every thing was exhibited which was likely to astonish him and elicit the latent feelings of delight, which must, unquestionably, have possessed his soul. So far from being in the slightest degree confused, he acquitted himself in a manner which surprised every one present. The faculty of imitation, which, as we have before noticed, he possessed in a high state of development, enabled him to copy the manners of those around him with such promptitude and precision, that it would have been difficult for one unacquainted with the fact to have told that he had been accustomed to move in a different sphere of life. The smile, the bow, and even the slightest gesture, he imitated with the most minute correctness. He expressed no astonishment at anything which occurred, until the table was exposed on the removal of the cloth; when, struck by its extent and beauty, he uttered an exclamation of surprise, and set about examining its structure and qualities.

That the propriety of Eenoo's behaviour on this occasion depended principally on his power of imitation, may be proved from the following circumstance : With the view of ascertaining how far his conduct might be attributed to this faculty, one of the gentlemen at the party purposely committed a breach of etiquette, and was immediately followed to the very letter, in his unusual course, by Eenoolooapik. But, being made aware of his error, and of the imposition which was practising upon him, without allowing his self-possession to be at all disturbed, he looked around, and after consulting the countenances of the various individuals, he readily concluded who he ought to imitate.

He was next taken out for a short distance to the country. He expressed himself as gratified with the appearance which it presented, and contrasted it with the aspect of his own sterile land. The trees, especially, astonished him by their magnitude; and he amused himself in measuring the circumference of several of them, and in comparing them with the stunted shrubs of the *west-land*—as he had been taught by the sailors to denominate the country of his birth. He displayed considerable anxiety to be informed concerning the nature of every strange object ; and, in return, he was very ready to communicate such knowledge as he possessed, in regard to the productions of his native clime, whenever an opportunity occurred for his doing so. It may be here remarked, however, that although he seemed interested about every thing which he saw, he maintained the utmost coolness and deliberation in examining whatever attracted his notice. The same perfect composure and gravity marked his intercourse with the various individuals whom he met; and, as yet, he was equally at home with every person, knowing none of the ordinary distinctions of society.

The change of circumstances which Eenoolooapik had undergone, was perhaps as great and rapid as can well be conceived. A month ago, and he had been among the fur-clad savages of Durban, a member of their tribe, and a follower of their customs ; and now, he was an object of attraction and interest in the midst of a civilized and refined community. It is difficult to imagine the process of thought which must have passed through his mind within this brief period; and his ready intelligence and perfect equanimity are still more curious and interesting phenomena. It might have been expected that one whose life had hitherto been spent amidst the bleak scenery of an arctic shore, where little save the bare rock, the withered lichen, or the eternal snow, meets the eye at every turn, would have been altogether bewildered by such a transition as that which Eenoolooapik had just experienced. There seems to have been a peculiarity in his case, which, perhaps, is

without a parallel. It is true there have been several interesting natives of distant climes brought
to this country on different occasions, who manifested
considerable intelligence and tact in their first intercourse with civilized society; but in what instance
is the contrast between the previous and after experience of the party so striking and singular, as in
the case of Eenoolooapik ? The isles of the Pacific
have sent of their sons to see the father-land of the
faithful missionary,—the dark children of Africa
have come to behold and bless the birth-place of
liberty to the captive negro,—the simple Hindoo,
and the stern Indian, may have trod our soil and
wondered at our science,—but all these had the re-
membrance of much that was lovely and luxuriant
in their own fair and fertile homes. Eenoolooapik's
memory had no such beautiful resting-places on
which to repose and expand itself. In the climes
of the south, nature is prodigal of her favours, and
lavish of her loveliness, and little would the inhabitants of such regions care for our richest landscapes,
if destitute of the decorations and trophies of art.
The towering cliffs of the stormy north may display
much of grandeur and magnificence, but the cheerless
snow-hut and the icy ocean can call forth few associations of repose, and could have done little to prepare Eenoolooapik's mind for the refinement into
which he had been ushered.

A few days after the arrival of the Neptune,
Captain Penny, at the urgent solicitations of his
numerous friends, allowed Eenoolooapik to display
his dexterity in the management of his canoe on the
river Dee. On this occasion he was with the greatest difficulty prevailed upon to exhibit himself in his
native costume; but so changed were his opinions
on the subject of dress, that he only did so, on being
assured that he would never be asked to put it on
again. The day happened to be exceedingly warm
for the season of the year; and Eenoo, ambitious of
shewing his expertness, exerted himself to the utmost
of his power. He became considerably overheated
in consequence of the severe exercise and the warm
nature of his dress, and the pulmonary affection from
which, as before mentioned, he was suffering, was
thereby aggravated. Its alleviation, too, was afterwards prevented by the imprudent manner in which
he exposed himself in the open air; for he resisted
every entreaty to remain in the house, unless when
Captain Penny was present with him. His disease,
however, at length assumed such an alarming form,
as not only to render confinement to his apartment
imperative, but even to threaten his existence.

Arrangements had been made for instructing
him in such elementary branches of education as it
seemed he was most likely to acquire with ease, and
also for teaching him the art of boat-building, which

E

it was thought would be highly useful to him. But the excellent and praiseworthy intentions of his friends were unfortunately frustrated by the very serious aspect which his malady had now assumed.

The disease from which he was suffering was an inflammatory affection of the lungs. It was extremely severe, but it presented no other remarkable peculiarity. The Esquimaux, even in their own country, are very liable to such affections during the summer months. They do not use any remedial measures, at least any which can properly be called so; but nature generally performs a cure by means of copious bleedings at the nose. They place implicit reliance on the powers of the *Angkuts,** who, when they visit a patient, bind up his eyes and utter some mystical sounds, by which, it is believed, they invoke the Great Spirit on behalf of the sufferer. The patient gets better in the way already noticed, and the Angkut receives the credit of the cure, and some substantial present for his services. Reared in the belief of the efficacy of their incantations, Eenoolooapik strongly objected to medical treatment; nor would he at all submit himself to it, until assured that it was the only means of saving his life. This

---

* The administrators of the superstitious rites of the Esquimaux, combining in their characters the professions of priest, physician, juggler, and *rogue.*

being strongly represented to him, he was at length persuaded to allow himself to be bled; but it was evident that he suffered the bleeding rather from the remonstrances of those about him, than from any idea that his disease would be subdued by such a remedy.

By the means adopted by his medical attendant, he recovered so far, that in about fourteen days he was able to leave his bed. He was now satisfied that the treatment which he had undergone had been of some efficacy ; but his faith in the Angkuts was not on that account in the least shaken. When speaking of their pretensions, he related that on some previous occasion he had been very ill, and an Angkut had been called to see him, who, as he said, attempted to cure him " by much talking ;" but he stated it as an *extraordinary circumstance* that *his* disease had not been quelled by the power of the incantation. He did not perceive that this case militated against his own belief, for he evidently wished to convey a very favourable idea regarding the success of the Angkut practice.

As soon as Eenoolooapik's health was sufficiently improved, he was taken out to spend a day at the house of a gentleman who had shown a great deal of interest in him. Here he rendered himself amusing by the representations which he gave of the winter employments of the Esquimaux. His ignorance of

our language prevented him from using it in expressing his meaning ; but his pantomimic representation
of the seal-hunting and similar pursuits, is said to
have conveyed to the minds of the beholders a very
lively conception of what he meant to describe. The
keenness with which he entered upon this exhibition,
produced so much excitement in his yet weak frame,
that a relapse of his complaint immediately followed;
and it was attended with even more alarming symp-
toms than had been manifested in his first attack.

He was already so much weakened by the deple-
tion which had been necessary to subdue his first
illness, that he was little able to bear the remedies
which were requisite in this new attack. For nearly
three long and weary months he was confined to his
bed,—his frame shattered, his strength wasted, and
his mental energies impaired. He was, in short,
brought to the very brink of the grave. After the
excitement which attends the earlier stages of his
affection had passed away, he sunk till his life trem-
bled in the balance. He lay motionless and apparently unconscious of what was going on around him.
His extremities were cold, his eyes sunken, and the
expression of his countenance ghastly—the powers
of nature seemed exhausted: yet he rallied ; but his
convalescence was protracted, and the slightest exposure tended to produce a relapse.

For a long time he suffered with the most exem-

plary patience, and not even a murmur escaped him;
but at length he became enervated by continued
pain, and the thought that he was dying began to
steal over him. He then displayed great anxiety
on account of his mother, and was much distressed
by the reflection that he would never see her again.
On one occasion this feeling operated so powerfully
upon him, that he cried bitterly, and reflected upon
Captain Penny for bringing him away.

This solicitude on account of his mother was nothing more than we should have expected, considering the duty which is required from an Esquimaux
to his maternal parent. Her support in old age entirely devolves upon him, and when deprived of this,
her condition is miserable in the extreme. Hence,
to be childless is among them considered one of the
greatest misfortunes imaginable; and when such
happens, it is common for them to adopt the children of others, in order that they may not be left
destitute in the evening of their days, when they
have become unfit for the active duties of life. The
practice in question prevails most extensively in regard to boys, they being most useful; but instances
are not unknown where girls have been adopted;
and even the exchange of children is not uncommon,
apparently for the purpose of preserving an equal
balance of the sexes in a family.

During Eenoo's recovery it was found necessary

to aid the prostrate powers of his constitution by means of wine and other stimulants. When this practice was first adopted he seemed rather averse to take them, but by and by his disposition towards them assumed a more friendly aspect. Having, apparently, discovered their cheering influence, he was in the habit of slipping out of bed, when unperceived, and tasting a little of the inspiring liquid. It was once or twice remarked that he shewed an unusual flow of spirits, but his previous habits having been exceedingly temperate, the cause of his exhilaration was never suspected. He was one day, however, caught in the act, which put an end to all doubt on the subject, and also to his private indulgence.

There was perhaps nothing uncommon in this temporary wine-bibbing propensity, but it will be allowed that in the following respect his taste was somewhat peculiar. It had been found necessary to administer castor oil to him on various occasions, and instead of loathing this nauseous draught, as is usual with patients, in this country at least, he was always willing, and even rather anxious, for its copious administration.

He was very observant of the means taken for the cure of his disease, and particularly anxious to learn the nature of the indications which the pulse afforded. He would narrowly watch till the physician

withdrew his finger, and then he would pounce upon
the pulse, as if fearful of losing the opportunity of
examining its mysterious indications.

Returning health brought back with it his old
feelings and associations, and hope with its ever-
cheering beam again illumined his soul, and caused
him to forget his recent sufferings. Indulging in
the anticipatious of future pastime amid the wild
crags of his wintry home, he one day asked what
time he was to get a gun which Captain Penny had
promised him. He was yet scarcely able to leave his
couch, and Captain Penny, thinking that it might
relieve the tedium of his weary hours, immediately
procured the fowling-piece for him. When presented with it he expressed himself highly delighted, and
after having examined it sufficiently it was set aside.
The following morning he was observed to be exceedingly languid, and apparently much worse. On
inquiry being made as to how he had passed the
night, he confessed that he had crawled from his
bed, and spent several hours in examining his gun ;
which he had been enabled to do at the window, in
consequence of its being moonlight at the time. The
bad effects of this imprudent exposure, however, soon
wore off, and his recovery went on progressively.

Eenoolooapik's illness was a source of the utmost
anxiety to Captain Penny, who had, without any
reservation, engaged to restore him to his friends in

safety. Indeed he had even gone so far as to promise, that if any evil befel Eenoo, he would deliver
himself up to be dealt with as they should think fit.
This engagement, although made in the best possible
spirit, was yet of very questionable propriety; for,
had Eenoo died, quiet and inoffensive as the Esquimaux generally are, we are by no means satisfied of
Captain Penny's safety, if ever he should have come
within the range of their power. But, altogether
apart from his solicitude on that account, the attention and kindness which he shewed to Eenoo during
his illness, were of a character which commands our
admiration, and does him the highest credit. He
watched and tended him while he lay sick and pow-
erless; he relieved the tedium and monotony of his
couch in convalescence; and, in short, he was, as
Eenoo himself expressed it, " all the same to him as
a mother." Nor can we dismiss this part of the subject without again noticing the assiduity and high
professional skill displayed by Dr Pirrie in his attend-
ance on Eenoolooapik. It has been already remarked,
that the case was of a severe and dangerous character,
and, of course, requiring prompt and energetic treatment—but beyond the ordinary obstacles to recovery,
there was the blighting influence of climate to con-
tend against.

We have already mentioned that it had been resolved upon to instruct Eenoolooapik in some of the

elementary branches of education, and also to give
him some practical lessons in the art of carpentry ;
but the illness with which he was seized on his
arrival, and which, as we have noticed, assumed such
a serious aspect, prevented these designs from being
carried into effect. On his health being now in some
degree re-established, the process of teaching him
to read was commenced. He mastered the alphabet
with great readiness, but here his literary attain-
ments terminated. He had evidently no relish for
such pursuits, for he could not perceive any advantage which would afterwards accrue to him from
the knowledge of letters. It was chiefly by this
prospective principle that he was guided in every
thing which he set about learning or acquiring., If
he did not see that the subject of study or acquisition
would be of future utility, he could not be persuaded
to bestow attention upon it. When any *toy* accidentally came into his possession, he would examine
it with great curiosity and care, but after discovering
that none of the practical purposes of life, so far as
known to him, could be served by it, it was soon
thrown aside as useless. On the other hand, if he
got any thing which he judged might afterwards be
turned to account in his own simple avocations at
home, he hoarded it up with the greatest eagerness.

With this indifference to literary study may,
however, be contrasted his partiality to drawing.

F

This peculiarity of his disposition must have resulted from the predominance, in him, of those faculties of the mind on which that art depends ; for we can scarcely conceive any thing which was likely to be of less service to him amid the desolate scenes of his arctic home. He had from the first shewn an aptitude in that art which, if he had remained in this country and received instruction, might soon have rendered him an adept in the use of the pencil.

The restoration of his health being now so far perfected as to allow him to be taken out, he was again introduced to every thing which was likely to interest or inform him, and he displayed the same readiness of comprehension which had previously characterised him in the examination of every thing which was new and wonderful. When his attention was directed to any strange object or piece of mechanism, if he had ever seen any thing bearing even the most distant resemblance to it, he would instantly refer to that, and state that what he now saw was " *siniagout,*" or " almost all the same." Frequently when any thing curious was shewn him, he would examine it without making any remark, so that it appeared at the time to have made little impression upon him, but he would afterwards revert to the subject, and ask innumerable questions concerning it. On one occasion he was taken to a manufactory and first shewn the cotton in its raw state, and then he was conducted through the various apartments of the establishment and shewn the changes which the machinery effected on the substance which he had first seen. When he found it brought into the condition of fine thread, he took hold of the wristband of his shirt, and asked if that was not " all the same?" He was several times taken to the theatre and other places of public amusement, on which occasions he seemed to enter with all his soul into the nature of the scene. The theatre, in particular, was a source of much gratification to him, for it seemed as if he fully comprehended the exhibitions, and could judge of the assumed character and language of the various performers. He stated that the Esquimaux have similar pastimes, but of course on a more diminutive and less refined scale.

Innumerable instances, such as these, might be adduced in proof of Eenoolooapik's intellectual acuteness, but we deem what have just been noticed as sufficient for the purpose of the present part of the narrative. We will yet have occasion to notice several other peculiarities of his character, as displayed in the scenes through which he passed ere he again reached his northern home; and we may also be induced to offer some remarks on his mental constitution, after we have bid him farewell on his native shore. At present we waive the subject, and hasten to notice the incidents of the brief period which preceded his departure in the Bon Accord.

The latter part of Eenoolooapik's residence in Aberdeen was not characterised by any occurrence of moment. He continued the same course of observation which he had pursued from the first, and no doubt added daily to his stock of knowledge. As his acquaintance with the world increased, he became more retiring and bashful in the presence of those with whom he was not intimate ; whereas, at first, he was equally pleased with and communicative to all. This change, however, did not go so far as to affect the propriety of his behaviour, which, from being simply imitation of the actions of others, had now become a habit with him.

Ever since his transference to the Neptune, he had been accustomed to the use of our food, which did not seem to be productive of any injurious consequences to him, although he had never even tasted any thing of a vegetable nature before. It would appear, however, from some circumstances observed during his illness, that animal food was best suited to his constitution, as it was given to him with decided benefit when he was in a condition very different from that usually requiring its administration. He was, at first, in the habit of taking his food in a half raw state, but in a short time his taste in this respect underwent a complete change, and he refused it

when presented to him in that condition, declaring
that it had got " *oko too little*," or " too little heat."
He shewed no disposition to engorge himself in the
manner so common among the Esquimaux, but on
the contrary he was exceedingly abstemious and
moderate. Indeed, he shewed none of those fierce
and ungovernable passions which characterise man
in his savage condition, but, on the contrary, he was
mild and gentle in his nature, and modest, and even
delicate, in his intercourse with female society. The
attention which he received from the inhabitants of
Aberdeen, and in particular from those of them
connected with the Neptune, both on his arrival and
during his residence among them, was not more
flattering to the dependent stranger, than honourable
and praiseworthy to the parties bestowing it. Of
their attention and kindness he seemed duly sensible,
at least he rewarded them with much deference and
respect, and general amiability of character. He
once or twice displayed some little bursts of self-will,
which owed their origin to over-indulgence during his
illness ; but these were of short duration, and soon
gave place to his usual blandness and equanimity.

He had learned to abstain from his usual amusements on the Sabbath, and, previous to his leaving,
he was taken to church, where he conducted himself
with the utmost propriety, and followed the external
ceremonies of the worship as if he had been accus-

tomed to them all his lifetime. His instruction in religion had also been prevented by his long and dangerous illness, and it is questionable whether he had any understanding of the forms and observances in which he so readily joined. Nor was there now an opportunity left for his information, as his mind had become so much absorbed by preparations for his return, that nothing was heeded by him which had not a reference to his approaching departure.

In consequence of the information which he had given, it was determined that the Bon Accord, whale-ship (to which vessel Captain Penny had in the meantime been appointed), should, in the course of her voyage, examine Tenudiackbeek, and test the truth of Eenoolooapik's statements; but from the Government having declined to afford any assistance in the matter, the owners of the vessel were obliged to abandon that as a primary object. Having agreed to accompany Captain Penny in the expedition, the writer now became personally acquainted with Eenoolooapik. The remaining incidents of Eenoo's history, and the various circumstances connected with the voyage, having passed principally under the writer's own observation, he may be allowed the privilege of occasionally expressing himself in the first person—a right which he may already in some instances have assumed, in virtue of an author's arrogance, without craving the indulgence of his readers.

As the time of Eenoolooapik's departure drew near, he assumed a more business-like air, and employed himself in collecting such things as he thought would convey to the minds of his countrymen some idea of the wonders he had witnessed; and also in providing himself with numerous articles which would be useful to him in his various pursuits at home, and much more efficient than any thing which the rude arts and limited resources of the Esquimaux could supply. We have said that the Government had declined to afford any assistance in bearing the expense of an examination of Tenudiackbeek. This statement, however, must be qualified by the following fact. The Lords of the Treasury placed twenty pounds at the disposal of Eenoo's friends in Aberdeen, for the purpose of assisting in procuring whatever might be considered necessary to establish him in his native country in more comfortable circumstances than he had formerly enjoyed. And well provided indeed he became, for no cost was spared by his friends in furnishing him with every thing that was useful or desired by him. Fowling-pieces, with powder and shot,—edge-tools, of various kinds,—culinary utensils,—and clothing in abundance,—formed part of his miscellaneous acquisitions.

Although he had experienced so much favour and kindness, he did not seem to feel any reluctance to leave this country, but rather looked forward to his departure with pleasure. But, indeed, this need not be wondered at when we think of the sickness and sufferings he had endured. He was fully sensible that the climate did not agree with him, as he was constantly annoyed with cough, and, in fact, his health was never so thoroughly confirmed as to shew that he was becoming at all acclimated. It is highly probable that he would not have survived long here, but would have fallen a sacrifice to the insalubrious influences of our moist, inconstant atmosphere, and have found a grave where he had come to worship at the temple of knowledge.

CHAPTER III.

THE time was now come when Eenoolooapik must forego the pleasures of civilized life, and exchange the comfort and gaiety, in which he had for some time lived, for the rude hut of the Esquimaux, and the equally rude companionship of its inhabitants. But these considerations, if they occurred to him at all, were counteracted by other and more powerful feelings; for he now shewed considerable anxiety to depart, and appeared quite disappointed when the ship was accidentally delayed beyond the time fixed for her sailing. When questioned as to whether he would ever return to Britain, he replied, " Wyte you, wyte you, me takkou," or " wait until I see,"—alleging, as a reason for his indecision, that he thought there was " too much cough" for him here. He was, no doubt, influenced too by the strong attachment to home, so remarkable in the inhabitants of those countries where Nature appears in her sternest aspect; and though to us his native region might seem cold, cheerless, and forbidding, it was yet endeared to him by association with his earliest recollections. The contrast which his residence in this country formed with the nature of his former life must have made a deep impression on his mind ; but, instead of breaking his attachment to his own land, or exciting a desire to remain here, it very fortunately produced the wish of communicating to his countrymen the knowledge which he had thus obtained.

The 20th of March was the time first determined on for sailing, but the prevalence of strong easterly winds caused the tides to " take off" so rapidly, that we were obliged to wait the following stream. It was therefore the 1st of April ere there was sufficient depth of water to float the ship. On the night of that date we put to sea, and on the 4th arrived at Lerwick, in Shetland ; whence, having completed our crew, we sailed on the 8th.

Eenoolooapik's long and dangerous illness had, as before stated, prevented that advance in his education which was so much to be desired ; and, as the season of his opportunity for improvement was rapidly drawing to a close, it was determined to afford him as much information as possible, during his stay in the Bon Accord. So soon as all our arrangements were completed, and all felt themselves at home, we commenced to instruct him in reading ; but the prevalence of strong westerly winds and rough weather, rendered our passage across the western ocean exceedingly tedious and uncomfortable, and produced a state of things unfavourable to his advancement.

On the 18th we had reached the 25th degree of west longitude, when an event of the most melancholy nature occurred. During the early part of that day it blew fresh, accompanied at intervals by heavy squalls ; and, as the day advanced, the breeze increased, rendering a reduction of sail necessary. In carrying this into effect, about 1 P. M. several hands were sent out to stow the jib. While they were employed on this duty, the ship plunged heavily into the sea, and a man, named George Thomson, lost his hold, and was swept away. The commotion among the men on the forecastle, shewed to the others on deck, that some unusual event had happened, and a piercing cry soon directed attention to the spot where the object of their solicitude had just emerged from the water. The rapidity with which we were sailing at the time, rendered fruitless any attempt made to assist him while passing ; but spars, and other light articles, were instantly thrown overboard, and means taken to stay the ship. She missed stays, however, in consequence of the heavy sea, and ere we could wear round before the wind, we had left him far behind. I watched him anxiously, and he struggled long, for the dark speck was seen on the

bosom of the rolling wave, until lost in the distance.
When we did succeed in overrunning the spot, no
vestige of him was to be seen—the waters had closed
over him for ever.

This lamentable occurrence cast a gloom over the
crew, nor was Eenoo unaffected. He often reflected
upon it, and it led him to speak of the casualties
which sometimes happen to his own countrymen
when their light canoes are taken by the rising
gale. He mentioned, that the Innuit entertained
the belief, that such of their tribe as were thus cut
off, were at once transferred to a state of bliss. On
questioning him farther regarding their ideas of a
future existence, he stated that the Angkuts had
informed him that they had frequently seen the
spirits of the departed, and that the pleasures in
which they revelled were essentially of the same
character as those they had enjoyed in this life. He
mentioned, too, that it was for this reason that, when
any of the Esquimaux died, the bow and spear were
buried along with the body, or thrown into the
nearest water. He seemed to have no idea of future
punishment, but he thought all would not be equally
happy. He believed that the body did not lose its
sensation when dead; and he said, that in consequence of this belief, the Esquimaux are very careful
in constructing their graves, lest the body should
in any way be incommoded or oppressed. The care

which they display in building and roofing their
sepulchres, had, on previous voyages, attracted my
attention ; but I had concluded that it was on account of the rocky nature of the ground preventing
their being interred in any other way. It was interesting to observe the manner in which he endeavoured to make himself understood on the subject of
the immortality of the soul. I did not understand
the Esquimaux expression for *soul* or *spirit,* nor
could he express it in English ; but after several
ineffectual attempts to make me comprehend him,
he succeeded by informing me that it was " something small—all the same as he was, but not *nook-
kee* or *shounook,*" that is, neither flesh nor bone.

On the 1st of May we fell in with numerous icebergs, although we had not passed the 38th degree
of west longitude. These are seldom found so far
to the eastward, but the long prevalence of westerly
winds sufficiently accounted for their being here in
the present instance. From observations made at
the time, some of them were found to exceed 100
feet above the level of the sea, which, according to
the usual allowance of one part above for nine below
water, gives an entire depth of 1000 feet. From
the fact of the mass floating with its broadest part
in the water, this calculation does not give its depth,
but simply the relative proportions of ice above and
below water.

These enormous masses, against which the sea broke and raised its spray high in the air, presented a spectacle of the most terrific grandeur. But if during the day they were a fit sight for admiration, in the night-time they formed a subject of the deepest anxiety. The barometer had fallen—the sky looked wild—the breeze, the first favourable one we had experienced, was fast freshening to a gale—and the ship, even under a great diminution of sail, was ploughing rapidly through the water—while the night was so dark that the danger might be too near to be avoided ere it could be seen. Every precaution was taken to guard against accident; hands were placed upon the foreyard for the purpose of looking out, and instructed to observe the strictest vigilance in their duty. The night of the 2d passed in sleeplessness, certainly, but without any occurrence of moment, and the day when it broke, though it lighted our path through the waters, shewed also an increase of our danger. Streams of ice, the remains of icebergs broken up by the fury of the waves, lay scattered around, and icebergs in greater numbers than before. The gale speedily increased to a tempest, and the sea soon rose in proportion, rendering it hazardous to run, while to lay the ship to, was a measure, if possible, to be avoided; because, should danger present itself suddenly, which was likely to be the case in the night, she would then be too little under com-

mand to afford a fair chance of clearing it. But
dangerous although it was, there was no alternative,
and the sails being all taken in, with the exception
of the close-reefed main-top-sail, the ship was hove to.
The following night was passed in watchful anxiety,
but the morning's dawn shewed neither ice nor iceberg, and during the day very few pieces were
passed. Night again came, and with it our fears
returned. A thick drizzling rain and hazy weather
added to its gloom, and rendered the darkness yet
more deep, and the sea broke so much, that it was
difficult to distinguish ice from the white crest of
the breaking surge. All that prudence, coupled
with the full knowledge of our critical situation,
could suggest in the way of precaution, was had
recourse to, and it was fortunate that we had been
thus guarded ; for, about midnight, an iceberg was
discovered so close under the lee bow, that for a
time it seemed impossible to avoid it. Indistinctly
seen through the almost impenetrable gloom, though
scarce a ship's length off, lay the mighty mass,
against which the huge waves, urged on by the fury
of the tempest, rushed every moment with terrific
violence, to be flung back from the encounter as
from a rock of adamant, again to mingle in · the
roaring abyss. Direct upon this we were driving,
and it was obvious to all, that a collision under such
circumstances would dash the vessel to pieces in an

instant. The utmost skill and decision were necessary to meet the danger of the moment, but the means of escape being taken with promptitude and energy, the ship providentially wore clear. It is almost superfluous to observe, that the most vigilant watch was kept during the remainder of the night, and day-break looked forward to with the utmost solicitude. On the following day the weather moderated, and, rounding Cape Farewell, we gained the entrance of Davis' Strait.

A great improvement had now taken place in Eenoolooapik's health. The cough had entirely left him, and he was fast regaining the olive complexion, which had faded considerably when he was in Britain. His spirits, too, were elated by being again in his native clime, and by often seeing objects with which he had formerly been familiar. Drawing now became one of his favourite amusements, and he soon attained a proficiency in this branch, exceeding our most sanguine expectations. His progress in writing too, which we had commenced to teach him, was highly respectable, but in reading he advanced very slowly; his imperfect knowledge of the English language being a constant obstacle in his way.

It had been determined, for the reason already assigned, that we should not, at first, proceed to the examination of Tenudiackbeek, but pursue the intricate and tedious route by the eastern coast and Melville Bay, to the fishing stations on the western shore. In the event of our not obtaining a full cargo there, we intended then to take advantage of the information which Eenoolooapik had given; or, should a successful fishery render this unnecessary, it was resolved to bring the ship to anchor in Durban harbour, and undertake a journey across the narrow isthmus which the Esquimaux had described as being there, and ascertain the existence at least of the reported sea. We therefore pursued a course which was likely to bring us to the edge of the ice about the 62d degree of north latitude, as is the custom with the whalers. This point we reached on the 12th May, and finding nothing to interest us, we left it, and proceeded to the northward. On the 16th we saw the east-land in the 66th degree, distant about 30 miles. The mountains still displayed one uninterrupted covering of snow, and even the lower land near the shore was for the most part white—the few uncovered spots which existed, and the dark faces of the precipices where snow could not rest, only serving, by contrast, to heighten the desolate nature of the scene.

Eenoolooapik had frequently expressed a strong desire to see the eastern coast of the Strait, and to satisfy himself whether its inhabitants were similar to those of his own country. The moment he beheld

H

it, he exclaimed that it was " all the same as the
west-land." A few days of variable winds and calms,
prevented us from approaching sufficiently near to
gratify him with a sight of the inhabitants. During
this interval he was exceedingly anxious, and not
only his waking thoughts, but even his dreams,
which he frequently communicated, bore reference
to the expected meeting. On the morning of the
18th we reached in towards the land, to the northward of Reef Coll, and many of the natives visited
us. Eenoo appeared to be considerably excited
when he heard of their coming, and, as soon as
they were sufficiently near, he hailed them in his
native language. On their coming on board, he
examined their canoes and fishing implements with
a practised eye, and declared them excellent ; but
he affirmed that the Esquimaux were much inferior
in point of personal appearance to their brethren of
the west side. He conversed with them, and seemed
highly delighted when they used expressions which
he understood, and whenever any difficulty occurred
to them in understanding him, he had immediate
recourse to the English language to explain himself.
He listened with great attention to one of them
reading some passages from the Esquimaux Bible,
and admired some specimens of their hand-writing
which were shewn him ; and to prove that in that
respect he was not behind them, he took a pen and

wrote his own name with great correctness, considering that a few weeks before he could not form a letter. He shewed them his drawings, which excited great astonishment and admiration. These feelings may, perhaps, have been the more readily excited in them, inasmuch as they seem, in general, to possess a pretty large development of the faculties on which such accomplishments depend, although, from their manner of life, they are almost precluded from improving them by cultivation. Eenoo now became anxious to master the little difference which existed between his language and theirs. The slow manner in which they spoke, struck him as highly ludicrous; and his talent for humour frequently led him to repeat the words after them, mimicking them with laughable correctness.

Proceeding northward, on the 20th we visited the Danish settlement of Leively, on the island of Disco, and the kindness of Major Fasting, the inspector of an extensive district, who resides here, afforded Eenoolooapik an excellent opportunity of estimating the amount of advantage resulting to the Esquimaux from the formation of settlements among them. He admired the various specimens of their workmanship shewn him, some of which were presented to him as patterns for imitation.

We had been unable to land immediately at the settlement, in consequence of the ice being still at-

tached to the shore, and so were under the necessity
of walking for some distance; but when about to
return, the Major kindly offered to send us back in
sledges. Apart from being spared such a rough
journey on foot, the novelty of the drive was a
sufficient inducement for us to accept the offer.
Two trains of dogs were accordingly yoked to their
respective sledges, and away we drove. We had
proceeded very pleasantly for about two miles, when
Eenoo becoming ambitious of passing the sledge
which contained Captain Penny, instigated the Dane
who was driving, to put the dogs to their utmost
speed. The whip was immediately applied, and
with such effect, that we were soon alongside of our
companions. A snarling took place among the dogs,
and produced some confusion when we were passing
a fissure in the ice ; the consequence was, that our
sledge was overturned, and its contents rolled into
the crack. Eenoo and the Dane being both accustomed to such occurrences, extricated themselves
without difficulty, and escaped with a partial wet-
ting. I was less fortunate, for, falling undermost, I
underwent a complete immersion; but in the scramble
I luckily got hold of the thongs which fastened the
dogs to the sledge, and held on until fairly dragged
out. The bath was by no means comfortable under
such a temperature—even Eenoo declared there was
" *ikkee* too much," or too much cold.

The settlement which we had visited stands on a low point projecting from the southern extremity of the island of Disco. It was originally the flag-settlement, and although it is now superseded in importance by others farther south, it still forms the residence of the inspector, who, as before mentioned, was at this time Major Fasting. The kindness of this gentleman to the Esquimaux under his superintendance, cannot be too highly commended. He informed us that he had sent several young natives to Denmark, for the purpose of being educated. One of these he intended for a clergyman, and another for a schoolmaster. He stated that the mental capabilities of the Esquimaux were such as to encourage the hope that they would attain proficiency in any of these professions. He took a great interest in Eenoolooapik, and conversed with him on several matters connected with the habits and opinions of the Esquimaux, particularly relative to their religious belief.

The nature of the rock on which the settlement stands is granitic gneiss, which seems to stretch across a part, at least, of the base of the island, as a kind of fundamentary rock. Above this an immense mass of trap forms the bulk of the island. It rises several thousand feet above the level of the sea, and presents that peculiar shelved appearance which often characterises that species of rock. This is best seen at the distance of a few miles from the shore, when the snow lodging on the horizontal parts of the shelf, contrasts strongly with the dark face of the perpendicular portion, and makes the appearance of a succession of steps still more distinct. The mountains are remarkable for their pyramidal form, and are in some places of extraordinary height—their tops being almost constantly enveloped in clouds.

From Leively we pursued our way to the northward, passing through the Waygatz,—a narrow strait which separates Disco from the mainland. We then entered North-East Bay, where a considerable quantity of ice was lodged, which rendered the navigation somewhat intricate. Here we were frequently visited by the natives, whose language Eenoo now completely understood, and he was constantly questioning them about their method of fishing, seal-hunting, and other pursuits. On the 26th we had penetrated the barrier which occupied this bay, and found a great extent of open sea to the northward. Falling in with whales off the Black Hook, in latitude 71°, we were induced to remain some days in the prosecution of the fishery; but our attempts proving abortive, in consequence of the condition of the ice, and, tempted by the extent of open sea, we again proceeded northward. While here we had an opportunity of ascertaining, more correctly than we had hitherto done, the number of whales which visit Tenudiackbeek—by causing Eenoo to compare them with what were then seen; and though to us they appeared rather numerous, he declared them to be comparatively *meekiouk*, or few in number.

On the 2d of June we had reached the Danish settlement of Operniwick, from which we had a few natives on board. Eenoolooapik stated that their language approached much nearer to his own than that of any of the Esquimaux we had yet seen. It was observed that as we proceeded northward the similarity between his language and that of the natives increased, and here they became so nearly alike as to cause him to remark the circumstance. It was, however, obvious at the first meeting, that they were merely different dialects of the same language.

After passing Operniwick, we found our progress interrupted by a formidable barrier, and on the evening of the 4th we made the ship fast to an iceberg among the Frow Islands. The weather had for some days been rather hazy, and consequently prevented us from examining minutely the state of the ice which impeded us. On the 5th it cleared up, and I accompanied a party sent to the top of a hill on a neighbouring island, to ascertain the appearance of the surrounding sea. The ascent was not only a difficult, but even a somewhat dangerous one; for the mountain was so steep as to be barely accessible,

while blocks of rock, loosened by the frost of ages,
frequently rolled from under our feet, and gathering
force in their descent, with the noise of thunder
buried themselves in the abyss below. On reaching
the top, we were amply recompensed for our arduous
journey. The sky was calm, cloudless, and beautiful; and, although it was midnight, the sun was
considerably above the horizon, diffusing a mild
yellow radiance over the landscape, and altogether
free from that dazzling glare which, with the reflection from the ice and snow, it at mid-day produces.
To the south-west the sea lay open and placid as a
lake, and nothing was seen on its still bosom save
here and there a distant sail. From north-west to
north-east the prospect was grand. One continuous
sheet of ice covered the sea, apparently unbroken,
save by a few lanes of water near the shore. Icebergs in vast numbers and of the most fantastic
forms, towered high in the air; while the sun's
rays, playing on their glittering sides, produced the
most varied and beautiful hues. Towards the
north-east the shore stretched out, barren, bold,
precipitous—its high cliffs capped with the eternal
snows, and stamped by the hand of Nature with the
impress of desolation. There may be rich and
luxuriant beauties in a tropical landscape, and the
mind in contemplating them may be filled with
pleasurable emotions, but they are "tame and domes-

tic" in comparison with the stern sublimity of a polar scene. Such, at this moment, I felt must be the case, on looking down upon the prospect beneath us.

The island over which we had travelled was composed of granitic rock, and on its very summit immense blocks of the same material, rounded and smoothed apparently by attrition, were placed on such narrow and elevated situations, that one was almost tempted to think that, were it possible, they had been put there by human agency. Very few traces of vegetation were observed, except some kinds of grass, and the moss and lichen, the invariable accompaniments of even the most barren arctic rocks.

Notwithstanding the formidable nature of the barrier which opposed our progress, we were able on the 6th to make some small advance, by towing the ship through a narrow channel which was opening out along the land. Proceeding in this manner, on the 8th we had reached within 20 miles of the Baffin Isles, and even in this short time so great an alteration had taken place on the ice, that there appeared to be a wide expanse of open sea around these islands. Two broad streams of ice intervened between us and this water; and these we immediately attempted to penetrate. While engaged in overcoming them, it came to blow strongly from the south-west, which forced the ice so rapidly against

the land, that we were soon completely beset, and
driving along with it. We were then off a point
named Cape Shackleton, from which a reef of rocks
extends for some distance into the sea. This reef was
looked at with considerable anxiety, as it lay directly
in the course of our drift, and the ship was utterly
uncontrollable. Fortunately we drove clear, although
the rocks were seen not more than forty feet off
where we passed them. A partial opening in the
ice, produced by the projection of the above-named
point, enabled us to extricate ourselves from the
first stream, and we immediately attempted to push
through the second; but here we were again beset,
and so quickly did the ice close around us, that
what a few hours before was open water to the
northward, was now entirely covered by ice. The
gale continued with little abatement for two days,—
the ice closing, if possible, yet more closely. A day
or two of beautiful weather succeeded, and the ice
began to loosen; but around the ship the pieces had
overlapped each other so much, and the frost and
snow, which had accompanied the gale, had so
completely solidified them, that we found ourselves
immovably fixed in a solid mass. Sawing seemed
to be the only means of extrication, and this was
rendered exceedingly difficult from the immense
thickness of the overlapped parts. Some idea may
be formed of the difficulty of the undertaking, when

it is stated that the nearest point to the edge of the floe was 1200 feet, and that, in many places, it was 30 feet thick. After sawing, or rather quarrying, for two days, we succeeded in liberating the ship, and again resumed our voyage to the northward. Under the influence of a smart northerly breeze, the ice opened considerably, and threading our way through intricate channels, we passed the Baffin Isles on the 14th.

We had now entered Melville Bay, a place much dreaded by the fishermen, and certainly not without good reason ; for, not only are the dangers which surround the path of the navigator in those seas assembled here in their worst form, but the result of the fishery has for some time back been almost entirely regulated by the time consumed in overcoming the obstacles which this bay offers. From its situation at the top of the strait, it forms a receptacle for the ice when forced up by a south-west wind. Under such circumstances it becomes rapidly filled, and such is the violence with which the ice rushes in, that the strongest vessel which the art of man can construct, if caught between the floes, is instantly crushed like a shell. A sheet of ice, varying in breadth from 20 to 40 miles, and attached to the shore, commonly occupies the bight of the bay for the greater part of the season ; and along the margin of this the fishermen seek their way to the northward. The edge of this land-floe, as it is termed, is seldom quite clear of loose ice, but with a northerly wind a narrow passage is opened up, by which the ships are enabled to proceed. In calm weather, too, the ice loosens a little, and, by dint of severe and often long-continued labour, considerable advance is made at such times. The ships are then dragged forward either by towing with the boats, or by the men attaching themselves by a rope and walking along the edge of the ice. On these occasions, the stir and activity which prevails, the cheerful song of the tars, the bright dazzling light, and the fineness of the weather, all conspire to present a scene of the most animating description.

Advancing in this manner, on the 17th June we passed the promontory called the Devil's Thumb, and on the 22d we had reached the latitude of 75° north. The wind then came from the south-west, and, by shutting the loose ice against the land-floe, debarred our further progress. The barometer had fallen considerably, and gave us reason to fear that it would blow fresh. Accordingly a bight in the land ice was selected as offering the best place of security for the ship. Into this we made fast, accompanied by a number of other vessels. The Bon Accord occupied the innermost situation, while ranged outside of her were the other ships, and, immediately under our tern, the Hecla, famed in northern discovery, lay moored. During the night it blew strongly, accompanied by heavy squalls and showers of snow—the ice pressing in with considerable violence. At seven A. M. on the 23d the gale freshened, and a heavy mass of ice bore directly down on the ships. A point of it caught the outermost vessel first, but by quickly sawing it off she escaped. The mass then grazed along the sterns of the ships, and, taking the Hecla on the broad-side, in a moment crushed her to pieces. So rapid was the destruction of that noble vessel, that many of the crew had barely time to escape with such portions of their clothes as could be instantly laid hold of. When first nipped she lay over on her beam ends, and with the utmost despatch her masts were cut away, in the vain hope that she would right again ; but the ice pursued its career, burying her beneath it.

Absorbing as this scene was, the great probability of our own ship sharing the same fate in a few minutes prevented us standing by idle spectators. All were busy in removing such articles as were most likely to be useful, or were most conveniently taken away. The ice, the source of our danger, was also the depository of our stores, and thither every thing was conveyed. Scarcely was this duty finished when our worst fears seemed about to be realized. The floe, after destroying the Hecla, caught the Bon Accord on the starboard quarter, while on the

same bow she was heavily pressed by the ships
already mentioned—they being forced against her
by the weight of the mass. Her larboard side rested
against the land-floe, which at this place was unequal
in its surface, thus increasing our chance of destruction. The cracking of the timbers,—the leaning of
the ship,—and the breaking of the casks in the
hold,—demonstrated most emphatically the severity
of the pressure. The oblique position into which
the ship was thrown was unfavourable for resis-
tance; but, although her destruction was deemed
inevitable, she sustained the pressure until the ice
broke and afforded her room.

During the time this scene had been enacting,
Eenoolooapik, who, although sufficiently familiar
with the ice, had never witnessed casualties from it
on such a grand scale, seemed a good deal agitated.
The bustle and confusion attending the removal of
our effects to the ice, prevented him for a time from
steadily fixing his thoughts on the danger of the
ship; but no sooner was this accomplished than,
ascertaining her perilous situation, he burst into
tears. Although this may appear weak, he was by
no means destitute of courage, for, during the voyage,
when allowed to go in his canoe in pursuit of the
narwal, or merely for his own amusement, we had
seen him brave the most imminent dangers with
fearless intrepidity. On the present occasion he

seemed to anticipate the helpless condition in which he might be left, should any contingency deprive him of Captain Penny's protection. However, when all danger was over, he assumed his usual composure, and set about collecting such articles from the wreck, as he thought would be afterwards useful to him.

The gale now gradually declined, and on the following day it was quite calm. The various crews lending their assistance, a successful attempt was made to reach the wreck of the Hecla by sawing off a portion of the ice. Most of the men's clothes were thus recovered, but unfortunately they also found access to the spirit store, from which they speedily extracted a large cask of rum. This rich prize was with the utmost despatch rolled upon the ice—the top knocked in with the first available instrument—and then a scene exceeding all description immediately followed. Every article capable of containing fluid was in immediate requisition, and when vessels of the ordinary description could not be obtained, they contrived to supply the deficiency by various expedients. One man, whom I saw, being unfortunate in procuring a drinking cup of any common kind, sat down upon a hummock of ice, and deliberately pulling off one of his large sea-boots, fought his way most stoutly to the cask, which it was no very easy matter to reach, seeing that it was surrounded by about 150 men;

but after a hard conflict he gained it, then filled his boot, and departed in triumph. Others might be seen using their hats as drinking utensils; and some again, with frugal foresight, secreting large stores in the boats belonging to their ships. One individual had been so busy, in this last respect, as to attract the attention and call forth the censure of his companions; and on returning for an addition to his stock he was without ceremony forcibly taken and dipped head foremost into the cask, which fully satisfied his rapacious appetite. It is almost needless to mention that these copious draughts quickly reduced them to the extreme of inebriation. As an example we may notice the case of a seaman who, I am sorry to say, belonged to the Bon Accord. This man had been sent along with others to perform some necessary duty on the ice, and within half an hour he was brought back in such a state of utter insensibility that his companions thought him dying, and requested me to see him. Thinking the case a very fit one for the application of the cold effusion, I had immediate recourse to it, and with such effect that, after applying the second bucketful, his senses were so far restored that he imagined he had fallen into the sea, and struck out lustily as if swimming. He clutched an oar which happened to be lying within the range of his movements, with the grasp of desperation, and called loudly to his companions

to help him out. I was congratulating myself on the
great efficacy of the remedy which I had employed,
when my attention was called to an operation of a
similar nature in course of performance on board
a neighbouring ship. The nature of its action was
the same as in the case which I have just detailed,
but the method adopted was much more ingenious,
and quite original. One end of a rope was fastened
round the body of the *patient*, the other passed
through a block attached to the fore yard-arm and
then descended to the deck, where it was arranged
in such a way that the individual embraced by its
opposite extremity could be raised and let fall suddenly into the water. Several seamen were working
this contrivance in a very energetic manner for the
recovery of a soporose companion, and, judging from
his struggles after each immersion, it seemed to be
highly effectual in restoring sensation. It was much
to be lamented that such a scene should have occurred
at all, although one could hardly forbear smiling at
some parts of the proceedings. But such is the
infatuation of many of our sailors, that whenever an
opportunity occurs for indulging in intoxicating
liquors, they will embrace it under whatever circumstances.

All danger being over for the present, our chests
were again taken on board the ship, which, in the
meantime, had undergone a temporary repair—large

K

beams having been placed across the hold for the purpose of supporting the injured parts. On the 25th a slight change enabled us to move the ship into a more secure situation, where a proper dock was cut out of the ice, and on the 29th a northerly wind produced such a change that we again commenced to thread our way along the edge of the land-floe. However, on the 30th it again blew from the south, and, after running so long as the ice remained open, we were once more obliged to make fast and cut another dock.

We had now reached the latitude of 75° 10′ north, and Cape York, which forms the northern limit of Melville Bay, could be seen in very clear weather. The position which we occupied was one that afforded an extensive view of the coast of this bay, and it appeared to me to be the most dreary and desolate which is to be witnessed even in those latitudes. In fact it is nearly one continuous glacier, with some dark naked rocks protruding from it here and there. It seems to be the source whence the icebergs are annually sent forth in great numbers, and, as might be expected, they are found here on a scale of great magnificence.

While coming up the Strait, but more particularly while in this Bay, I had numerous opportunities of witnessing the remarkable effect of refraction. Objects which, from their distance, would not have been visible under ordinary circumstances, were seen high in the air, sometimes quite distinct in all their parts, at others broken and distorted, and frequently altogether inverted. This peculiar state of the atmosphere is such, at times, that no object without the range of two or three miles can be seen in its real form. A ship, at this distance, will sometimes present a singular appearance—the hull perhaps appearing to occupy its proper position in the water, while the topsails seem considerably elevated in the air and quite detached from the hull, and the top-gallant sails still more elevated and separated from every other part. On examining this for some time the appearance of things suddenly changes—all the sails becoming apparently united, but stretching upwards to a great height; or the hull may appear to assume gigantic proportions, and the masts and sails to dwindle into the most dwarfish forms. The coast, when viewed through the atmosphere in this state, presents, as Captain Scoresby has remarked, the appearance of " variegated basaltic columns ;" every rock seems drawn out into a column, and the appearance is repeated several times, so that columns seem to be arranged in tiers, one row standing immediately above another, or there may be a vacant space intervening between them. It would be vain to attempt a description of all the varieties of form which objects present when the condition of the atmosphere which gives rise to this curious phenomenon exists, for these are endless. But, besides being a matter simply of curiosity, refraction is of signal importance to the northern navigator, as it frequently points out to him the existence of open sea at immense distances, and by its indications his course is often guided.

At the northern extremity of this Bay, the extraordinary phenomenon of red snow is seen. There have been three conjectures advanced respecting the cause of this singular appearance: some attributing it to the existence of a microscopical plant belonging to the class *Cryptogamia*, and the natural order *Algæ*, and forming the species *Protococcus Nivalis* of Agardh, and the *Uredo Nivalis* of M. Bauer—others conjecturing it to result from the presence of innumerable minute animals of the order *Radiata* —and a third party supposing it to be produced by the ordure of the little auk, a bird which abounds on the rocky shores of the Arctic Seas.* In 1837 I had an opportunity of walking along the shore in the neighbourhood of some high cliffs which presented a crimson aspect, resulting from the presence of this wonderful substance. It then appeared to me that the snow upon the shelves of the rocks and

* Ed. Cab. Lib. vol. i. pp. 106–9.

at the foot of the precipices, where it exhibited a
deep red colour, owed this to the immense numbers
of birds which had their lodgment there. But in
many places, especially in the valleys, the snow had
a rose tint, which had no appearance of having been
produced in the same way, and it is highly probable
that it resulted from the presence of those minute
plants. It is impossible, without a very narrow examination, to determine accurately the cause of this
appearance; but from whatever cause it results, if I
might judge from the pleasure with which I myself
beheld it, one of its uses seems to be to relieve the
eye, wearied with the continual glare of those vast
fields of snow. Speculations about final causes have
been denounced as inimical to the interests of true
science; but surely it may be a legitimate exercise
of reason, and in nowise prejudicial to sound philosophy, to trace the evidences of the Deity's beneficence as displayed in the numerous arrangements of
nature. Thinking so, and feeling so, I cannot but
remark that the eye, dazzled by the intense light
which obtains over those snowy wastes, turns with
avidity to, and finds relief in, a scene of such soften-
ing and soothing beauty. With what delight must
the Esquimaux, who are so passionately fond of
red colours, gaze upon this singularly beautiful phenomenon! May it not, then, be one of those beautiful adaptations of nature which prevail in every

department of creation, and tell so powerfully and
intelligibly of the wisdom and beneficence of the
Great Author of all.

CHAPTER IV.

A PROFITABLE voyage can seldom be secured by visiting the fishing banks on the western coast after the beginning of July. This season was now at hand, and such was the condition into which the ice had been brought by these repeated gales, that there was very little chance of our being able to penetrate it at an early period. It was therefore determined that, should it not open before the 10th of that month, we would, if possible, extricate ourselves and proceed to the southward for the purpose of examining Tenudiackbeek. This resolution was farther strengthened by observing that the rest of the ships were already seeking their way out. However, the ice remained so close about us, that before the day appointed for leaving we should have found it impossible to move; but on that date it opened a little, and we commenced our return. Previous to this time all the ships had left, with the exception of five sail, which were moored in the same floe with the Bon Accord.

One of these now accompanied us ; the commanders of the others deemed it prudent to remain, in the hope, perhaps, that an early change might yet enable them to penetrate the barrier in time for the fishing.

Although the course now determined on was one which would soon restore Eenoolooapik to his friends, yet he was reluctant to relinquish the hope of a passage being effected to Agumiut, as he termed the northern part of the west coast. The same spirit which had actuated him in visiting Britain, produced also the desire of being made better acquainted with those parts of his own country which he had not visited. Indeed, he seemed to possess in a high degree those faculties of mind which phrenologists have adduced as finding their legitimate exercise in the observation of the relative situation, extent, and peculiar appearances, of places. He also took particular delight in copying maps and charts, and in pointing out upon them such places as were familiar to him ; and, although he was ignorant of the mathematical principles of geography, he could delineate with remarkable precision the actual direction of any coast, and the true position of its different parts. He could trace the course which we had taken across the Atlantic, and would, at any time when asked, point out the proper bearing of any place which we had visited.

On the 12th we again passed the Devil's Thumb,

and with little difficulty reached the open water, which by this time extended to the Baffin Isles. It was deemed necessary to run close along the great body of ice which occupied the middle of the Strait, and to follow its sinuosities for the purpose of ascertaining whether it at any point presented an opening leading to the westward. Off the above-mentioned Isles it appeared loose, and an attempt was immediately made to penetrate it ; but, when about forty miles off the land, an unfavourable wind forced us again to seek the open water. From this point down to latitude 66° we examined it minutely, but nowhere did it offer the slightest inducement for us to attempt a passage. In the last-mentioned latitude we saw the west-land, distant about forty miles. The intervening ice, however, was very heavy, and altogether impenetrable.

Eenoolooapik felt deeply disappointed at our not being able to reach the land in the neighbourhood of Durban, in order that he might obtain information regarding his mother, of whom he said he had been thinking much lately. It seems that the Esquimaux hold the opinion that " coming events cast their shadows before," for he believed that these thoughts were the presentiments of some evil which had befallen her in his absence. On attempting to rally him out of this opinion, he replied that " the Innuit were all the same."

If he had ever entertained any thought of returning to Britain with us, it was now evident, from the
manner in which he employed himself, that he had
abandoned such intention. He would still read or
draw when asked to do so, but he preferred over-
looking the operations of the cooper and carpenter,
and spent a good deal of his time in constructing
apparatus for his future avocations. He anticipated
the impression he would make on his countrymen by
the information he would have to communicate to
them, and stated that when the winter's storm confined the Innuit to their huts, he would entertain
them by a relation of the many things he had seen.

He now underwent repeated and severe examinations regarding Tenudiackbeek, but he firmly adhered to his former statements. Indeed, had not
anxiety for the result of the voyage prompted these
questionings, there was no reason, from anything we
had seen of him, to doubt what he had said, for he
was remarkable for his strict adherence to the truth.

On the 27th we had reached the latitude of 65°,
and were able to approach within about ten miles of
the shore, near the point named Saunderson's Tower.
We found the land to terminate abruptly here, and,
although it was again seen to the southward, it
appeared to be not less than seventy or eighty miles
distant. This was a state of things which we were
by no means prepared to expect, for in the ordinary

charts the shore is laid down as being continuous to
the southward until it reaches Cape Enderby, which
forms the northern extremity of Cumberland Strait,
in latitude 63° 15′. Finding an inlet of such magnitude, the idea instantly occurred to us that this
might be the entrance to Tenudiackbeek, and Eenoo
was immediately called upon for his opinion. He
accordingly went aloft, and after a careful examination declared it to be as we had supposed. Correct
observations being made, the ship's latitude was
determined to be 65° 1′; thus proving that this
spacious inlet was not the entrance to Cumberland
Strait, but a place hitherto undiscovered. To this
Captain Penny gave the name of Hogarth's Sound,
in compliment to William Hogarth, Esquire, of
Aberdeen, whose kindness and attention to Eenoolooapik, when there, rendered him so well worthy
of the honour.

The ice was much narrower here than at any point
we had previously visited, but it was still sufficient
to prevent our entrance into the Sound. It was
not, however, considered so formidable but that the
first strong wind from the west might disperse it.
We therefore resolved to wait for a change, and to
examine it from time to time, to ascertain whether
any alteration had taken place.

In making these examinations we were much
annoyed by the thick fog which almost constantly

prevails near the confines of the Arctic Circle during the summer months. This fog is said to be produced by the cold ice and water condensing the moisture with which the warm winds from the south come up loaded: or by the cold wind from the north condensing the vapour which arises from the comparatively warm water in the latitude of which we are speaking. In the bays and inlets, and indeed for a few miles all along the land, there is sufficient heat accumulated to enable the atmosphere to hold the moisture in solution, and the sky is therefore commonly quite clear in such situations.

On the 31st it blew a strong breeze from the south-east, which, although not in the most favourable direction, had the effect of so dispersing the ice that on the 2d of August we were able to run within the entrance of the Sound. Beyond this a barrier still occupied its entire breadth, but we were in high hopes that, by watching the tides and taking advantage of the partial openings which they produce, we would soon be able to overcome it.

During the gale above-mentioned we had accidentally parted from the barque Truelove, Captain Parker, who had accompanied us in the hope of making a fortunate voyage. But, when the weather cleared up, we descried two vessels in the offing, which we recognised as the Lady Jane and Lord Gambier, both of Newcastle. Concluding that these vessels

also were in search of this place, in consequence of
Eenoolooapik's report respecting it, we made a signal
for them to follow us, lest they should pass on to
Cumberland Strait, which was then supposed to be
the entrance to Tenudiackbeek.

A nearer view now enabled Eenoolooapik to re-
cognise many places on the eastern shore, within a
few miles of which we were; and he particularly
pointed out one place named by the Esquimaux
Tuackduack, which he had long before informed us
we should find to bear a very exact resemblance to
Cape Searle. So striking indeed was the resemblance, that all who had seen the last-mentioned
promontory at once perceived the similarity. He
was not, however, so well satisfied with the western
shore, for he seemed to think that it should have
been farther distant. This we supposed to arise
from his having seen it formerly out of the oomiak,
when close to the east side, whereas he was now not
only nearer to it, but also much more elevated, and
the weather remarkably clear.

The eastern coast stretched to the north-north-
west, by compass, for about forty miles, when it
terminated in a projecting point, which we named
Cape Crombie, after Mr Crombie, owner of the Bon
Accord. This coast, so far as it was visible, was, as
Eenoo had led us to believe, high and ironbound,
excavated by a few bays, and having some small

islands interspersed along it. It was almost completely clear of snow, but exceedingly naked and barren.

After passing two days (during which we were joined by a few more vessels) in examining the barrier which opposed us, it was determined to push into it and work our way through by warping This proved to be an undertaking of the most arduous description; for, though on the first day we made considerable progress, being aided by some partial openings and a fair wind, on the second we were completely beset; nor did our utmost endeavours suffice to advance the ship a mile through the ice. But it was observed that we were driving rapidly up the Sound, in consequence of the tide running with greater strength and for a longer period to the northward than it did in the opposite direction. We had also made the important discovery that there was a broad sheet of water within the barrier, and the knowledge of this stimulated us to still greater exertions.

Eenoolooapik displayed the utmost anxiety to overcome the obstacles which opposed us. He worked at the capstans—an exercise for which he had hitherto shewed no great inclination. His usual amusements were almost entirely laid aside, and if requested to read or write, he would answer that there was too much ice. A spare moment he would sometimes snatch to decorate his canoe or fishing apparatus with paint, or to examine his *eeclameek*, as he termed his chest. These examinations were conducted with the greatest secrecy, and it was a mark of the highest confidence to be present at them. On one occasion, while thus employed, he was disturbed by somebody approaching, and in his haste to replace the articles which he had been looking at, he set fire to his clothes by stooping over a candle that he was using, and narrowly escaped being severely burned.

Five days of almost incessant toil brought us to the edge of the ice, and on the evening of the 10th we got into the open water, near the point which was afterwards named Queen's Cape. During this interval we had enjoyed the most beautiful weather, which was fortunate, as we were completely at the mercy of the ice. It also allowed us to delineate carefully the coast along which we were struggling, and to determine accurately the situation of the different points we passed.

We had scarce reached the water when we were visited by two natives whom we had seen laying in wait for us. These being taken on board, Eenoo recognised one of them, having seen him at Durban. The other had never before seen a human being differing from his own tribe. He began to evince his surprise by shouting and leaping, but

Eenoo not relishing this behaviour on the part of his countryman, recommended him to desist. This he did until presented with a large knife, when his joy was beyond restraint. He put the point of it to his tongue, their invariable method of examining such objects, then uttered a yell of savage exultation, leaped, and waved his arms wildly in the air. To make amends for this exhibition, Eenoo instructed him to thank Captain Penny, which he did, uttering the word *Quinameek* with such frequency and force, that we were fain to put a stop to this expression of his gratitude. They brought off from their huts, which were on the shore of an adjoining bay, some whalebone and numerous walrus tusks. They informed us that the whales had been very numerous during the summer, and they thought that we would still find them plentiful in Kingoua. They put many questions to Eenoo regarding what he had seen, but we were obliged to cut short the dialogue, in order that we might take advantage of the fair wind which was then blowing. Before their departure, however, we requested them to communicate to the neighbouring tribes information of Eenoo's return, by which means it was hoped the news would reach his mother.

After rounding Cape Crombie we found the land to trend to the northward very nearly as Eenoolooapik had described it. We stood over towards the

opposite shore, and in the morning passed Keimooksook, Eenoo's birth-place. We then steered directly
up the Sound, keeping rather nearest to the western
shore, and giving names to the most prominent
points.

About mid-day, when passing through a stream of
ice, we discovered four natives sitting on one of the
pieces, with their canoes drawn up beside them. On
seeing us approach they launched their skiffs into the
water and came towards us. Eenoo was requested to
invite them on board, as we were anxious to learn
what they knew concerning the whales. When they
came near he looked at them with a little surprise,
but without speaking. One of them, however,
quickly recognised him, and called out Eenoolooapik! Eenoo immediately responded in the same
manner by repeating the name of the one who had
addressed him, and asked them to come on board.
He then informed us that two of them were cousins
of his own from Keimooksook. They were aware of
Eenoo's having visited Britain, but they shewed not
the slightest emotion on meeting him, and no greet-
ing of any kind passed between them, farther than
what we have described. When questioned regarding the whales, they stated that they had seen them
very numerous, on the previous day, a little to the
south of Keimooksook; and they advised us to return
to that part, but they at the same time mentioned that

M

they believed we would find them still plentiful in Kingoua. They all agreed in stating that the latter place was the principal resort of the fish; and it was therefore thought best to proceed to it at once. They informed Eenoo that his mother was well, and that, fearing that the ship would not reach Durban in consequence of the ice, she was coming round to Keimooksook, where she supposed he would be landed. This information gave him great satisfaction, as he was very fond of his mother; indeed, she was the only one of his kindred to whom he was at all attached, and we felt rather disappointed at not having an opportunity of witnessing their meeting.

Eenoo related some particulars of his voyage to his cousins, and it was observed that among the first things he told them was the manner in which the Esquimaux of the east-land spoke. He shewed them the fowling-pieces he had brought along with him. These they viewed with much surprise, and their use being explained, they expressed a wish to have their power tested. A mark was accordingly hung in a convenient situation, and, after seeing Eenoo fire, one of them was persuaded to try it himself. He was a little timid at first, but at length he took the piece and fired. He seemed vastly pleased when he saw that he had hit the mark. They shewed us some splendid archery—one of them, in particular, repeatedly putting an arrow through a hole about an inch in diameter, at the distance of about seventy feet. They advised Eenoo not to return to Britain, and, had Captain Penny consented, he would have left us and gone with them then, but we had further occasion for his services. They remained on board until taken about fifty miles from home; and, indeed, they shewed no wish to leave us, but becoming concerned for their safety, we were obliged to dismiss them. Before departing they received a few presents from Eenoo, on which they shewed a tendency to evince their gratitude in the manner of those of our first visitors; but Eenoo was considerably displeased at their want of decorum, and instantly interfered to repress their extravagance. At length they went away apparently highly delighted with the treatment which they had received.

Pursuing our way up the Sound, in the evening we were opposite the place which the Esquimaux named Kingaïte. To this the name of Beaufort's Inlet was applied. The channel was now becoming narrower, and numerous small islands were seen stretching across a considerable part of it to the northward. The western coast, of which we had obtained a very good view, answered Eenoo's description well, as it seemed to be a complete maze of islands— the mainland being seldom seen. These islands were barren and naked, but being completely free from snow, they had a rather milder appearance than the eastern shore, which was still bold and craggy. The weather was so warm and beautiful that, but for the occasional streams of ice which we encountered, we could scarcely have supposed ourselves navigating an arctic sea.

We now began to feel very anxious about the fishery, for, though we had passed some very fine streams of ice, no whales had been seen. The greasy appearance of the water, and the peculiar odour which it emitted, shewed that they had lately been there in vast numbers; and so high were our hopes of making a successful voyage, that immediately on getting clear of the ice we made preparations for the fishing on a large scale.

On the evening of the 11th we stood over towards the eastern side, and in the morning were within a few miles of the land. A great number of small islands seemed almost to shut up the passage to the northward, but, among numerous openings, Eenoo-looapik pointed out one as leading to Kingoua, of which we were then in search. The navigation of it, however, was much to be dreaded, as there seemed to be numerous sunk rocks and reefs, and we were anxious to fall in with some of the natives, as they are generally very well acquainted with the situations of these hidden dangers. We at length descried four natives in their canoes passing between some islands, but they appeared rather inclined to avoid than to approach the ships. Eenoo was therefore despatched in his canoe for the purpose of bringing them on board.

At this moment our attention was attracted by a circumstance which I must here pause to notice. Mr Jamieson, the Surgeon of the Lady Jane, had accidentally received a gun-shot wound which had proved fatal, and this was the time chosen for the interment of his remains. The half-hoisted ensign, and the boats leaving the ship with their colours lashed down, apprised us of the event, and I took a boat and accompanied the melancholy procession. The day was calm and exceedingly beautiful, and nature herself seemed pensive and sad. We landed on a point which looked as if formed for the resting-place of strangers from a milder clime. It was a smooth verdant platform, and at this time smiling with flowers,—an Eden in the wilderness,—forming a pleasing contrast with the naked sterile rocks all around, and seeming to tell of a heavenly paradise of permanent rest and bliss, when the rugged paths and bleak storms of this life are all passed and over. A high rock rose abrupt and precipitous from the green and flowery spot—a grand and enduring monument to mark the grave of the unfortunate youth. It was a moment of deep feeling and interest, for, though no father, or brother, or kindred, were there, to " lay his head upon the lap of earth," there

were not wanting kind and affectionate hearts to
sigh over his solitary resting-place, as we bade a
silent farewell to the hallowed spot. His name will
be perpetuated where his ashes rest, for the towering
cliff, at whose base he was buried, was by common
consent denominated " Jamieson's Monument."

On returning to the ship I found that Eenoo had
induced the natives to come on board. Their canoes
were loaded with whalebone, which seemed to be
from an animal very recently killed. They stated
that the whales had been very abundant until the ice
broke away from the land, after which they gradually
disappeared. They still, however, held out hopes of
our getting some in Kingoua, and with a degree of
caution which was not to be expected from them, they
recommended, through Eenoo, who acted as inter-
preter, that we should not enter that place with the
ship, in consequence of the tide running with great
rapidity through the narrow parts of the inlet. It
was therefore determined to seek a harbour for the
ship, and send an exploratory expedition in boats
for the above purpose. Very fortunately, excellent
anchorage was discovered close to the entrance of
the inlet, and the ship was immediately brought up.

On the shore of this harbour was situated the
Esquimaux village of Noodlook. The whole inhabitants, men, women, and children, were speedily on
board the ships, and the presence of Eenoolooapik

rendered the Bon Accord a centre of attraction.
We were first visited by the male part of the popu-
lation in their canoes, then came the oomiak containing the women and children, under the guidance
of an old man; and a most active and noisy traffic
immediately ensued. They were all aware of Eenoo
having been to Britain, and they crowded round him
to learn the particulars of his voyage. In relating
some of his adventures he chiefly addressed himself
to *Coonook*, the adopted daughter of Aaniapik, the
old man mentioned before as guiding the oomiak.
The features of this girl were naturally of a pleasant
cast, and on this occasion they were more than
ordinarily attractive. Since coming on board her
face had been washed, her jet black hair combed,
braided, and decorated with ribands; and, in short,
she displayed such a profusion of charms as immediately won the regard of Eenoo. It soon became
evident, from his behaviour towards her, that she
was acquiring a powerful influence over him, and
had any doubt remained upon the subject, it would
have been dispelled by seeing the severe rubbing of
noses which took place between them—such being
the manner in which the Esquimaux testify their
affection towards each other. This was followed by
a request, on the part of Eenoo, that I would immediately marry them, *all the same as the Kudloonite.*
Not having, however, taken holy orders, I declined

officiating on the present occasion. Eenoo, love-sick
as he was, did not on that account resign himself to
despair, for many long conferences might be seen
taking place between him and Aaniapik, the result
of which was, that, provided Captain Penny consented, Eenoo was to give his green painted canoe
for the beautiful Coonook, and this canoe was to
become the property of Aaniapik's youngest son, he
himself being unable from the infirmities of age to
manage it. Captain Penny being at the time engaged with other more important matters, the circumstance passed over without his attention.

It may be remarked that this affords an illustra-
tion of the Esquimaux ceremonial of marriage.
Presents are offered to the parents of the lady, and
if accepted, the matter is considered as settled. These
contracts are sometimes entered into at a very early
age; but it would seem that, on arriving at maturity,
the parties may break the engagements under certain circumstances. Coonook had been betrothed to
another when a child, but the importance which
Eenoolooapik had acquired by his visit to Britain,
was considered sufficient to nullify any previous
engagement.

On the morning after our arrival at Noodlook,
Captain Penny set out on his exploratory expedition
to Kingoua—Aaniapik and Eenoo accompanying
him. The former had gone principally for the

purpose of bartering a quantity of whalebone, which
was still attached to the animal on the spot where
it had been dragged on shore.

During the day I visited the village and inspected
its arrangements. It consisted of seven summer huts,
which, from the migratory habits of the Esquimaux,
were necessarily of a very portable description. Two
poles with their ends resting upon the ground, and
inclining till they met at the top, were placed for
each end of a hut. These were connected by another
laid along between them for the purpose of supporting the roof. A covering, made of seal skins sewed
together, was laid over this frame and fastened to
the ground by means of stones placed along its border.
One end of the hut was close, at the other the covering was disposed like a curtain, which served as a
door. These tents formed the only protection of the
Esquimaux during summer; and indeed I have seen
them sleeping in the open air, with no other couch
than the hard rock afforded, and no covering save the
blue vault of heaven. The outside of some of the
huts was rather neat, but an examination of their internal economy was by no means so satisfactory. The
lamp commonly stood on the middle of the floor, and
the skins used for bedding, articles of dress, and
pieces of seals' flesh, and other substances for food,
were strewed carelessly around. The utensils in
which they prepare their food, when they find it

N

convenient to give it any preparation, were composed of stones hollowed out in a very neat and ingenious manner. Their lamps too were of the same material, and the wicks were formed of dried moss. Many of their articles were constructed with considerable ingenuity, but every thing was shockingly dirty, and little or no order observed in the arrangement of their domestic affairs. Outside the huts, a number of the junior members of the community were amusing themselves riding on the dogs, and by such other sports as seemed to them best. A few boys, apparently about ten years of age, were sitting astride a rock and working vigorously in the water with a paddle; and I understood that it was thus they were first taught the use of that instrument, in working which they afterwards acquire so much dexterity. A party of older Esquimaux were occupied in alleviating the pangs of hunger by devouring the boiled carcass of a seal. As I approached they made room for me to sit down, and invited me to join in the repast. Of their proffered hospitality I, however, declined to partake. They suffered no interruption in their meal, but went on at a rate which threatened quickly to exhaust the supply before them. Turning from these, I walked on to examine a very small hut which was situated a little apart from the others. It seemed to be incapable of containing more than one person, and what was still

more singular, it appeared to be quite close, with the
exception of a small hole at the top. My approach
apparently disturbed the inmate, for a head suddenly emerged from the aperture, and I was not a
little surprised to discover that it belonged to the
fair Coonook, whose charms had made such an impression on our friend Eenoo on the preceding evening. I was about to address her, when one of the
Esquimaux touched me on the arm and requested
me to assist him with the oomiak, which the others
were now employed in hauling upon the beach. I
easily understood that this was meant to divert my
attention, as there were more around the oomiak
than were required to move it; and the thought
immediately flashed upon my mind that the girl was
under a periodical separation, like that recorded of the
Jewish females in Sacred Writ. It appeared to me
somewhat singular that a custom forming part of the
prescribed ordinances of the Mosaic economy should
also obtain among the unenlightened savages of the
Arctic Zone. I need not say that I paid instant
respect to the delicate and ingenious manœuvre of
the Esquimaux, and immediately retired with him
to the party at the oomiak.

At the period of our visit there were about forty
inhabitants at the village, but they stated that during winter their number would be much increased—
the majority of their tribe having gone to the lakes

(of which there were many not far distant) for the purpose of catching salmon. There were also numbers of them inland at the deer-hunting.

The practice of tatooing their faces is universal among the females after marriage, but very few cases have come under my observation where it was done before that auspicious event. From this circumstance, we had no difficulty in distinguishing those who had been at the Hymeneal altar. Whatever notions the Esquimaux might attach to this custom in respect to its adding charms to their female partners, it appeared to me to have a very opposite tendency even in youth, and in old age it is perfectly frightful. In this process they do not depict any regular figures, but simply make straight lines. These commonly diverge from the lower lip and angles of the mouth like rays, and one proceeds up the ridge of the nose, and dividing, extends over each eyebrow.

The Esquimaux here informed us that the preceding winter had been unusually severe, and that many of the neighbouring tribes had suffered dreadfully from famine. So awful had been their condition, that they were driven to the horrible alternative of eating the body of one young man who had died. The huts of these unfortunate creatures were seen standing lonely and deserted on a neighbouring island, and the yet unburied remains of their former inhabitants lay scattered around.

On the morning of the 14th, Captain Penny returned to the ship. He had been about forty miles up the inlet, but his search after the whales had been completely unsuccessful. At every place he had visited he found confirmation of the statements of the Esquimaux regarding the number in which the fish are at some seasons to be found there. Bones were to be seen strewed on the beach in every direction, and at the place to which Aaniapik guided them, they found a very large fish which had been killed about ten days before. It was supposed that there were not less than twenty tuns of blubber piled upon the beach at this point. Near the same spot there were also the remains of former victims in great abundance. From the top of an adjoining hill they could trace the continuity of the land all round; but as there was no prospect of better success in the discovery of the whales, they went no farther, but returned to the ship.

In the course of this expedition they had seen some of the natives who inhabit the shores of this inlet. From them they learned that for some days back no whales had been seen, but the Esquimaux observed that if they would wait until the sun was low they would find them again very plentiful.

Old Aaniapik, who, as before mentioned, accompanied Captain Penny up Kingoua, was so much excited by the recital of Eenoo's adventures, that,

though tottering on the brink of the grave, he began
to entertain the wish of also taking a voyage to
Britain, and he had confidentially told Eenoo, that
if invited to accompany us home, *he* would not make
any objection. He seemed to think that, in consequence of his former acquaintance with Captain
Penny (whom he had seen at Durban), he had a
perfect right to do what he pleased on board, and
being a harmless creature, he was not interfered with
unless he shewed a wish, which he sometimes did,
to appropriate to himself some small moveables to
which he had no title whatever. These thefts were
commonly committed quite openly, and Eenoo's in-
terference speedily produced a restoration of the
stolen property.

He was a great favourite with the sailors, who
had nicknamed him Commodore Timothy; and to
make his appearance correspond with his title, they
had dressed him in a blue jacket and canvas trowsers,
with a cocked hat profusely decorated with red
tassels. In this guise he strutted about with great
dignity, and seemed to think himself fit only to be
admired. He presented such a ludicrous figure in
the uniform in which the sailors had invested him,
that I was induced to attempt a sketch of his appearance; but I was severely punished for my rash
performance. Eenoo noticed what I was about, and
having a leaning towards the venerable Aaniapik on

account, perhaps, of the lovely Coonook, and feeling
besides for the honour of his countryman, and kind-
ling to think that he should be the sport of an idle
penciller, repaid me, with interest, in a most wicked
caricature, which would have baffled even Cruik-
shank to have made more comical.

I have already spoken of the pretensions of the
Angkuts in reference to curing disease, but it may
be here remarked that their power is only supposed
to extend to internal and obscure affections. Severe
injuries from external violence, such as wounds and
fractures, are of common occurrence among the Esquimaux, as might be expected from the perilous
nature of their pursuits. Experience has taught
them that the incantations of the Angkut avail not
in such cases, and in these they have therefore
adopted a different and more rational mode of cure.
The treatment of such injuries is entrusted to those
to whom long years have brought experience and
wisdom. Such was old Aaniapik, and the great
ingenuity which he displayed in his practice deserves
particular notice. I had first met him at Durban
in 1835, and at that time I had a case of fracture
under my care. He came on board the ship shortly
after the occurrence of the accident; and on learning its nature, he immediately went ashore, and soon
returned bringing with him some dried salmon skins,
which he instructed me to soak in water until they

became quite soft, then to wrap them one by one round the fractured limb, and allow them to harden in that situation. Although I did not think fit to follow his advice in the treatment of this case, yet the ingenuity of the plan, and the great similarity which it bears to a practice sometimes adopted by surgeons in this country, struck me forcibly. On making further inquiry into the matter, I found that this was not their only method of treating fractures. In some cases they use splints and bandage, but they err in allowing the patient to move about during the cure; hence their practice is not always successful. On that occasion Aaniapik requested my advice relative to a disease of his eyes, which, on examination, I found to require a trifling surgical operation. He submitted to this without scruple, and, for the time, it was productive of the desired effect. On meeting him at Noodlook in 1840, I was disappointed to find that his disease had returned, and, indeed, it threatened soon to deprive him of sight. I advised him again to submit to the operation, but, though he readily consented, he shrunk from the application of the knife, and I was ultimately obliged to desist from the attempt. It is painful to think of the wretched condition which would soon be the fate of poor Aaniapik. Day by day his sight was becoming more impaired, and rendering him less fit for the duties which were still required of him ; and erelong total blindness would render him unable to contribute in any way to the welfare of the community, when his state would be one of unalleviated misery. When the fierce blast of the winter storm rages along those desolate shores, and sweeps with resistless fury across the frozen surface of the deep, famine often reduces the miserable inhabitants to the extremity of distress, and the old and infirm are neglected and allowed to starve. Such would be the portion of poor old Aaniapik, and such is the fate of many in that rigorous clime—cast off in their infirmity from the sympathies of kindred, and left to perish without help or hope.

CHAPTER V.

WE had up to this time entertained the most sanguine expectations of making a fortunate fishing in this place; but now, after Captain Penny's return from Kingoua with no better prospect, our hopes forsook us. But, although mortified at our want of success, it was some consolation to think that Eenoolooapik had practised no deception towards us. We had everywhere met with abundant testimony of the truth of what he had stated, and it was evident that his information might have been turned to good account had the examination of the Sound been gone about in an earlier part of the season. In saying this, however, I do not mean to animadvert on the conduct either of Captain Penny or the owners of the ship. The fishery in Hogarth's Sound had not yet been tried, and the evidence of its existence rested solely on the word of Eenoolooapik. The Admiralty, as before mentioned, had declined to afford any aid in the matter, and it was scarcely to be expected that

the owners of the ship would, on the word of a
stranger and a barbarian, venture on an untried
field of enterprise, without some assurance of indem-
nification in case of failure ; and as regards Captain
Penny, he pursued the only course which prudence
warranted. He took the precaution of first attempting the fishing by the usual route, but, finding that
impracticable, he returned with the view of testing
the correctness of Eenoolooapik's statements respecting the existence of Tenudiackbeek, and its capabilities as a whale-fishing station. His perseverance
in investigating the facts connected with the Sound,
and his strenuous exertions to render the voyage
prosperous, must be already apparent, and require
no comment from me.

Our attention was now turned to the place to
which Eenoo's cousins had at first directed us, and
it was therefore determined that we should again go
southward. On the evening of the 14th a light
breeze enabled us to leave the harbour. For two
or three days we made but little progress—the winds
being light and variable. The navigation under
these circumstances was rather critical, from the
very strong tides which run in the upper part of
the Sound rendering the ship unmanageable when
surrounded on all sides by low islands and sunken
rocks. A smart breeze at length came from the
south, which, though it laid us under the necessity

of plying to windward, afforded us an opportunity of examining and delineating the shores more correctly than we could do in running up. The name of Davidson's Inlet was given to Kingoua, after another of Eenoo's friends in Aberdeen, and that of Bon Accord was applied to the harbour in which we had been. Appellations were also bestowed on such other places as, from their situation and appearance, were deemed worthy of names.

On our passage down, Eenoo entertained us with the relation of various circumstances connected with the different points which we visited. He related one event of a rather calamitous character that had occurred on a low island which we passed. A family of Esquimaux had encamped there during the winter, and constructed their huts on a low point near the shore, when the tide, raised by a heavy gale, forced up the ice, surprised them in their sleep, and buried them all beneath it, with the exception of one poor woman, who escaped destruction at the time, only to perish afterwards by cold.

Our examination of the coast to the south proved, so far as our success in the fishery was concerned, equally unsuccessful with our investigations in the north. Now and then, when we were able to penetrate to any distance among the islands which are crowded along the western shore, we saw some small whales, but they never presented themselves in situations favourable for their capture. The Esquimaux could give us no information where the whales had gone to, but we inferred from the above circumstance, that when the ice leaves the Sound, some of them at least seek shelter among those islands, whither it is impossible to follow them.

On the 20th, being close to the land within a few miles of Keimooksook, we were visited by about sixty of the natives—great numbers of whom were related to Eenoolooapik. They were the finest tribe we had hitherto seen; and Eenoo's near relations in particular were much superior in point of personal appearance to the rest. Eenoo informed us that one of his cousins was chief, or, as he expressed it, captain of the tribe. There seemed to be but little difference between the chief and the others; nor could I ever learn what was the nature of the allegiance they owed him. Eenoo was anxious to accompany them on shore, and as there appeared to be no probability of our being able to land him at Durban, it was considered a fit opportunity for allowing him to leave us. The authority of his cousin would, it was thought, secure him from any ill treatment; but, indeed, we had no occasion to fear such at the hands of his countrymen. We were by this time quite satisfied concerning the safety of his property; for we had seen that though they would steal from us whenever they had an opportunity, yet among themselves they practised

the strictest honesty. And even on board the ship,
when they coveted anything, it was sufficient to say
that it belonged to Eenoo, and they would instantly
let it alone.

Eenoolooapik's education was now so far advanced that he understood the method of convey-
ing his thoughts in writing, and for some time back
he had been contemplating writing a letter to Mr
Hogarth. Although the resolution which he had
formed of immediately departing with his countrymen left him little time for this purpose, neverthe-
less, he set about it and produced the letter, of
which we here present our readers with a fac simile,
and a translation ; as, besides being a literary curiosity, it will enable them to judge of the rapid
progress which he had made in that department of
learning. The little time now left him necessarily
rendered the letter brief; much more so, indeed,
than he had at first intended. A few days previous
to the time of which we speak, he had drawn out a
scroll of what he intended to introduce; and, although
we cannot publish that document, it may not be un-
interesting to notice its contents. After acquainting
Mr Hogarth with his arrival, and his intention to
remain at Keimooksook, he proceeded to draw a
comparison betwixt the condition in which he would
live there and that to which he had been accustomed
while in Aberdeen. He dwelt particularly upon the

Mr Hogarth

Tenudiackbut moacbut

unuckbock kimudoomote Eenoolooubit

Ackkelib vakuk ackuckaumenguckbkooruk

ookuckut pelackmeeum takenkohwuerkasunga

-laralooutebock Ennungite ockbakeluack-but

Pedeuackbanga Cap.ᵗⁿ Benj.ⁿ guilurite Ennuet

uneubout tauane tamokoanname pedeuurranga

Eenoolooubit.

The above of which the following is a translation was written on board the Brig Record

Wisgarth's hand 22th August 1816.

Mr Wisgarth:

Eenodoorpik has moved on Tenudoolook and intends to remain at Heimerbeck:

The Innuit say that for many saw the whales were very numerous, but before the ship came they had all disappeared. They also say that the whales will return when the sun leaves too?

Captain Penny has been very kind to me and to many Innuit, who all thank him. That is how you were kindest to me other I was with you.

Eenodoorpik.

filthy habits of the Esquimaux and the miserable
huts in which they live, as compared with the ele-
gance and comfort of the apartments which he had
seen and lived in when in this country. But though
he thus shewed that he knew the full extent of the
sacrifice which he was making, he stated it as his
firm determination to remain in his own country, at
least for the present. He mentioned, however, that
should a favourable opportunity occur, at some future
time he might be induced again to visit Britain.

We may be apt to think that he shewed a strange
and unnatural predilection in thus choosing to forego
the advantages of civilized life, and return to the
barren haunts of his early childhood ; but let us only
think of the deep and uneradicable associations that
cluster and cling around the *home* of our own early
years, and our surprise at Eenoolooapik's resolution
will be qualified. It was Nature's earnest promptings
that urged him to return to the land of his birth ;
for, dreary and desolate though it might appear to
others, its snow-clad hills and craggy cliffs were to
him as the faces of familiar friends ; and, besides,
there were the strong and enduring claims of maternal relationship binding him to home—principles
which, we have seen, reigned paramount in his
ingenuous nature when laid on a bed of languishing
and apparent death.

I have already mentioned that his long and severe

illness while in Aberdeen had prevented any steps
from being taken for his instruction in religion.
During the voyage, I had repeatedly endeavoured to
convey to his mind some idea of the nature of the
Christian system, and had attempted to convince him
that the incantations of the Angkuts were mere impo-
sitions. I succeeded in making him understand that
our belief was very different from his, and also that it
was derived from the Bible. More than this I cannot say that I accomplished. My limited acquaintance with his language rendered it impossible for me
to express myself in an intelligible manner; neither
could he understand me when I attempted to explain my meaning in English. I frequently read
and assisted him to read portions of the Scriptures
translated into the Esquimaux language, and used
at the Danish settlements on the eastern side of the
Strait; but there were many difficulties in the way of
his understanding these also. We often came to
words and passages which he could not at all understand, and on such occasions he stated that these
passages were not "Innuit speak." After reading a
passage, I was in the habit of making him attempt
a translation of it into English; and he sometimes
succeeded wonderfully. As an example we may
give the 19th verse of the 1st chapter of Matthew,
which, without assistance, he translated from the
Esquimaux as follows :—" Joseph, by and by her

husband, a very good man, wanted to put her away when nobody see." Notwithstanding that he assented generally to our superior intelligence, he would not be convinced that the Angkuts were impostors. But, indeed, there was nothing in this but what might naturally have been expected of him, for it would not have been reasonable to have given up his belief at a mere bidding, especially when we could not, from the difficulties already detailed, instruct him in any other doctrine. A copy of the Scriptures, which his friends in Aberdeen had procured for him, translated into the Esquimaux language, was left in his possession, but it is scarcely to be expected that he could succeed in understanding it with the slender literary acquirements which he possessed. He stated that he would speak of it to the Angkuts ; and on one occasion he asked whether, after we got to the Sound, I would *try* them with the Bible. This appeared to me to be an indication that he had some vague apprehension of its nature, and, had time and proper assistance been allowed him, I have little doubt but the mists of superstition which clouded his mind would have yielded to the purifying and enlightening influences which accompany the reception of Christianity into the soul.

About 5 p. m., all being in readiness for his departure, a small skiff was presented to him, and in it his effects were stowed, at least so many of them as

P

it would hold, for he had collected an immense
quantity of indescribable articles. He then left the
ship amidst the cheers of the crew, with all of whom
he was a great favourite—his Esquimaux brethren,
in their canoes, Captain Penny, Mr Allan the chief
mate, and myself, accompanying him. When we
landed we selected a sheltered spot and erected a
hut for him to spend the night in, as he was not to
proceed to the settlement until the following morning. A few of his relations agreed to stop with him
all night, and the rest of the Esquimaux encamped
on a small island close at hand. Every thing being
arranged to his entire satisfaction, we shook hands
with him and bade him farewell! He shewed not
the least emotion at parting with us, but after returning our farewell cheer, with the utmost *sang
froid* turned about after his own business, " nor
cast one longing lingering look behind." This is a
trait of character common among the Esquimaux ;
but as I am now to offer a few remarks upon the
characteristic qualities of Eenoolooapik's disposition,
I will merge the description of this peculiarity of
the race in the review which I take of his mental
constitution. I do not mean to advert to the whole
of Eenoolooapik's mental character, but only to the
more prominent features of it as displayed in the
various situations in which we have seen him placed ;
and in doing so we may see how far these faculties

are in harmony with the circumstances by which he had been surrounded.

The best marked feature in his mental constitution was the ample development of those faculties on which the attainment of geographical knowledge depends; and it will be recollected that the first circumstance which attracted attention to him at all, was the extent of his acquirements in that department. The facility with which he had acquired this knowledge is apparent from his having only *once* sailed between Keimooksook and Durban along the coast, the features of which, after a long interval of time, he described with such remarkable accuracy. I am inclined to believe, not only from my own observation, but also from the accounts given by Parry and others, that the Esquimaux generally possess the mental faculties necessary for this attainment in a pretty high state of perfection; and when we consider that they are forced from their situation to derive almost their whole subsistence from the sea, and often obliged for this purpose to undertake long journeys, and necessarily migratory in their habits— the necessity for such observational capacities appears abundantly obvious. The readiness, too, with which Eenoolooapik acquired the power of communicating this knowledge—his using rude sketches for the purpose of making himself understood when language altogether failed him, and the fondness which he

shewed for drawing, all afford additional evidence
of the activity of the same elementary faculties of
mind acting in a different manner in consequence
of the difference of his situation. Again, the development of several of these faculties, combined
with constructiveness, is strongly illustrated in the
ingenuity and neatness displayed by the Esquimaux
in the construction of their canoes, fishing apparatus,
and articles of dress; and it was probably this
combination which enabled Eenoolooapik so readily
to comprehend the various mechanical contrivances
which were shewn him. When we reflect on the
little that nature has done for the Esquimaux, and
the great ingenuity required to construct from the
slender stock at their disposal the means necessary
for procuring subsistence, we cannot fail to see the
vast importance of possessing such a mechanical
talent.

The faculty of imitation which, as we have before
mentioned, Eenoolooapik possessed in a very high state
of activity, is rather different in its nature from those
we have just noticed, and would, at first sight, appear
to be rather a useless quality; but it would have
been an extraordinary circumstance to have found
in him a faculty highly developed which had not
been subservient to some important end. Accordingly we find, on looking more narrowly into the
habits of the Esquimaux, that this power is common

among them, and is of signal consequence. By possessing it they are enabled to imitate the cries of the various wild animals which roam over those trackless wastes, and thus to bring them within the range of their seldom erring shaft. It was no doubt the exercise of the same faculty, directed to a different purpose, and combined with a pretty large endowment of self-respect, which enabled Eenoolooapik to conduct himself with such propriety on his first introduction to civilized society. His fondness for theatrical amusements—his comprehending the representations with readiness—and his disposition to humour and caricature, are evidently all traceable to the combination of the imitative power with secretiveness and wit, which existed in his mental constitution, and the general activity of the intellectual faculties, which distinguished him above many in civilized life.

The thievish disposition of the Esquimaux is matter of notoriety, and seems to indicate a great want of concientiousness; but Eenoolooapik evidently possessed a greater share of this sentiment than generally falls to the lot of his brethren. For, though he carefully collected whatever was likely to be useful, in no instance did he display a wish to appropriate what he had not the clearest title to take. The same sentiment was also manifested in his strict adherence to the truth. His love to his maternal parent has been frequently referred to in this narrative, and was a trait in his character which might be copied with advantage by many reared under more favourable circumstances. But, while he exhibited this pleasing trait in common with the rest of his countrymen, he also shared with them in that obtuseness of feeling which leads them to look with indifference on the happiness or misery of all others around them. He met his relations and native acquaintances, and parted with us, without the slightest emotion. Yet he had evinced many commendable qualities, and, on the whole, had much that was amiable about him ; and, perhaps, had his intercourse with society, where the higher sentiments are cultivated, been of longer duration, this apathetic disposition might have been modified. It is pleasing to think that, in visiting this country, he has learned nothing that will tend to degrade him. On the contrary, we may hope that his residence among us may have imbued his mind with some noble principles which may tend to soften the remaining barbarity of his nature, and in the evolution of Time's dark mysteries, become subservient to the good of the hyperborean races. Under the influence of these bright hopes, we bid him— Farewell !

Having disposed of Eenoolooapik, we proceeded to examine the state of the ice at the entrance of the Sound, in order to determine whether we could

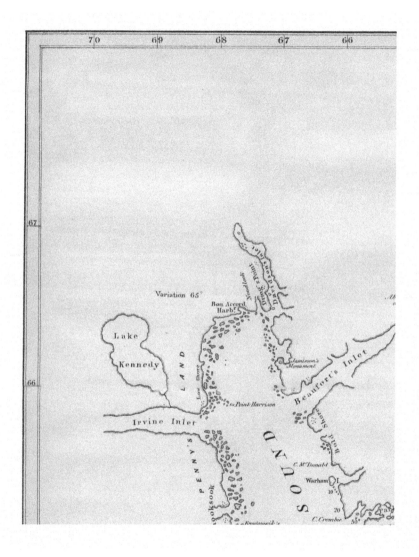

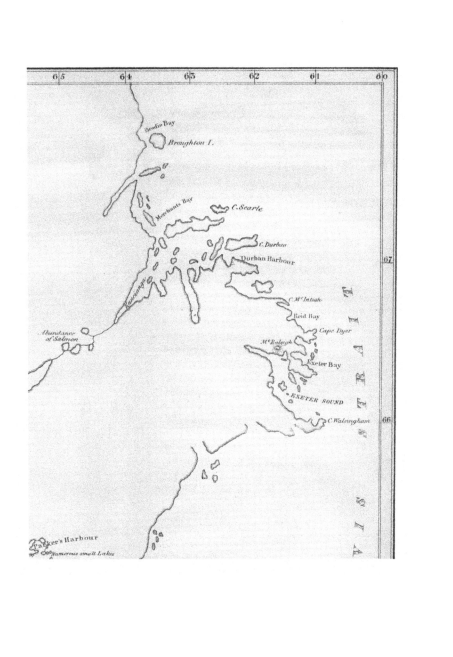

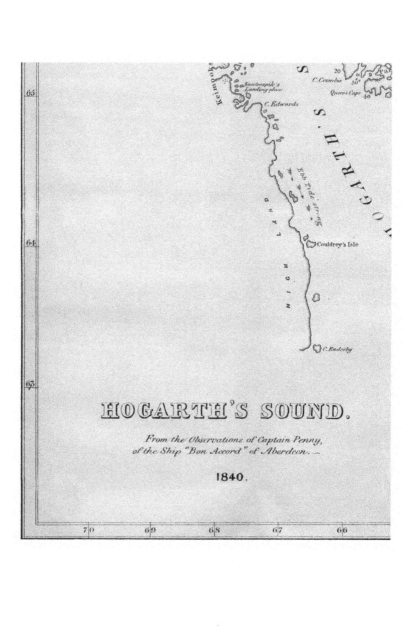

HOGARTH'S SOUND.

From the Observations of Captain Penny,
of the Ship "Bon Accord" of Aberdeen.

1840.

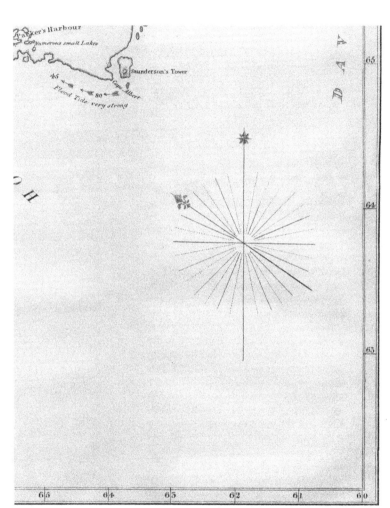

Parker's Harbour

Numerous small Lakes

Saunderson's Tower

45

80

Cape Albert

Flood Tide very strong

D A V

H O

65

64

65

65

64

65

62

61

60

easily reach the sea when we should find such a
course necessary. We had the satisfaction to observe
that there were only a few streams, which we might
easily penetrate, between us and the outside. But
a very slight examination sufficed to shew that the
ice was, if possible, still more closely packed along
the coast of Davis' Strait; and hence it was evidently hopeless to make any attempt to proceed
again to the northward in that way. Nothing therefore remained for us but to wait patiently until the
time when—according to the information given by
the Esquimaux that the whales would come when
the sun was low—we expected to find them con-
gregating in the Sound.

Having satisfied ourselves regarding the state of
the ice, we again entered the Sound, and steered
close along the western shore until we arrived at the
point where we landed Eenoolooapik. The name
of Penny's Land was given to the coast at this point,
in compliment to Captain Penny, senior, a gentleman
who had for very many years commanded a whale-
fishing ship. We had thus completed the examination
of the shores, and on reviewing the chart which we
had constructed (and of which we here insert a copy),
it was found to bear a close resemblance to the delineation given by Eenoolooapik. Almost the only error
worthy of notice was the situation of the entrance;
and this, as before mentioned, can scarcely be called

a mistake of Eenoo's, as it was merely supposed, from the reason already mentioned, that it communicated with the sea by means of Cumberland Strait. His utter unacquaintance with the mathematical principles of geography, and his ignorance of the coast farther south, rendered it impossible for him to give certain information on that point. The description which he had given of the direction and appearance of the coast was fully verified, and abundance of proof everywhere presented itself of the correctness of his statements regarding the fitness of the Sound as a whale-fishing station. Scarcely a canoe came alongside the ship but contained some remnant of the animal; and we had ourselves witnessed the remains of several whales which the Esquimaux had killed during the summer. Even if these positive proofs had been wanting, the great abundance of animalculæ in the water would have led us to believe that whales frequented the Sound. In some parts the water presented the peculiar olive-green colour, which Captain Scoresby has shewn to depend upon the presence of incalculable numbers of minute animals (*Medusæ*); and it is well known to every experienced fisherman that the whales are found in greater abundance, and rest better, in such situations than where it exhibits the oceanic blue. On some of these banks, as they are termed, I have observed the water to present a brown muddy-like appearance, resulting perhaps from the presence of a different species of the same animal.

As the season was now far advanced, and the weather becoming unsteady, it was thought advisable to seek a harbour for the ship, where we would be able to prosecute the fishery in a much more certain manner than by keeping the open sea. In the course of our search after a good anchoring place, we had occasion to revisit the neighbourhood of Keimooksook, and we expected to have an opportunity of again seeing Eenoo. In this, however, we were disappointed, for the Esquimaux informed us that he had gone inland on a hunting expedition, and would not return for some time. They likewise stated that he had been *married* since our departure, so that it seems his passion for the fair Coonook had been as evanescent as it was sudden; unless, indeed, he still entertained the idea of taking her also— such things being quite common among those in authority among the Esquimaux, as in all probability Eenoolooapik would soon be, from the importance which would be attached to his visit to Britain.

Not having found a convenient haven on the west side, we stood over towards the eastern shore, and on the 4th September discovered a very good anchorage, in which we brought up, accompanied by the Truelove, and were soon afterwards joined by se-

Q

veral other vessels. We were now much gratified
to find the accounts of the Esquimaux confirmed,
by the whales beginning to make their appearance;
and the boats were sent out every morning to watch
them as they coursed close along the land. So long
as the weather continued fine, a good many fish were
seen, and two or three captured by some of the ships
in company. However, we were not so fortunate,
for, after harpooning two large animals they were
both accidentally lost. But the weather soon completely broke up, and gale followed gale with so little
intermission, that the boats could seldom be sent
away; and when taken by the breeze, at a distance
from the ship, they were sometimes obliged to run
for the first place which offered any shelter, and to
remain there, exposed to the tempest, till it moderated. Indeed, so sudden and fierce were these
breezes at times, that on one occasion our best boat
was driven upon the rocks, and dashed to pieces with
such rapidity that the crew had barely time to save
themselves; and several boats belonging to other
ships fared the same fate at the same time. Under
these circumstances it was scarcely to be expected
that any success could attend our endeavours; yet
we were reluctant to relinquish the attempt, so long
as hope could be entertained.

The harbour being at no great distance from the
encampment of the Esquimaux, whom we had seen

on first entering the Sound, they soon discovered our
situation, and removed their huts for the purpose of
being near the ships. They consisted, in all, of about
thirty individuals, without, so far as I could discover,
any chief or superior among them. They had mi-
grated from Tuackduack, the head-quarters of their
tribe, to the locality where we had first seen them ;
as it was a place very favourable for the capture of
the walrus, and there were also numerous lakes in
the neighbourhood which supplied them with abundance of salmon. During our stay they carried on
an extensive traffic with the ships, and no doubt
obtained many things which would be highly useful
to them. But the principal benefit which they
derived from the presence of the ships was the car-
cases of the few whales which were captured. They
cut large portions of the flesh from these, and buried
it beneath a pile of stones, to prevent the encroach-
ment of beasts of prey. In consequence of this store,
they determined to establish their winter quarters
in their present situation, and I observed them
making some burrows in the ground over which
they intended to construct their snow habitations ;
as yet they sought no protection but the skin huts,
though the weather was very cold and stormy.

I have had frequent opportunities of observing
the physical peculiarities, manners, and customs of
these primitive tribes, both in Hogarth's Sound and

around the entire circuit of Davis' Strait, and they present such a uniformity of character, that the description of one tribe will, with a very few trifling exceptions, suffice for all. The following remarks therefore, though drawn from the little community that for the time inhabited the shores of this harbour, may with equal propriety apply to the whole.

In the configuration of their bodies they present well marked characters of Mongolian descent. The figure of the head is rather square, the face broad and flat, and the features run so gently into each other, that they do not appear abrupt or distinct. The forehead is small, but not remarkably so, and the space between the eyes large. The eyes are dark and placed obliquely, the external angle being turned upwards. The eyelids approximate very closely at the outer canthus; at the inner, the upper eyelid joins the lower by a gradual turn. In some cases the obliquity of the eyes is such as to produce a very striking resemblance to the Chinese countenance; but in many others this peculiarity is not very obvious. The cheeks are very prominent and rounded, the nose broad and flat, and very little depression between it and the cheeks. The upper lip is long, the lower is thick and projects slightly. The lower jaw is thick and strong, and its angle very prominent. The teeth are regular, but the tubercles on the crowns of the molar teeth are very indistinctly marked. The hair

is lank, black, and strong; and is worn long by both
sexes, except immediately over the forehead, where
it is cut short in the males. The beard is generally
scanty and confined to the chin: in some few cases
I have seen it copious, but it is frequently altogether
wanting. The skin is of a light olive colour, smooth,
and destitute of pilar hair. Its colour is heightened,
but not produced by their filthy habits, as it exists,
although in a very slight degree, at birth; and it
never becomes so deep as to obscure the rosy colour
of the cheeks in young females. The chest is capa-
cious and well formed. The extremities are short,
and the hands and feet exceedingly small. The
average height of the male adult Esquimaux is about
five feet four inches. Their limbs are soft and
round, the muscles are flaccid and not well marked.
Such are the physical peculiarities which charac-
terize these tribes; but, though a general similitude
prevails throughout the whole, yet a narrow inspec-
tion will readily enable an observer to discover
minute shades of difference between the different
members of a community, which serve to distinguish
them from each other.

In their moral and intellectual qualities, this particular tribe differed in no respect from the neighbouring hordes; and, as we have already noticed
their principal mental peculiarities, in connection
with those of Eenoolooapik, it is unnecessary again

to repeat them. But it may be here remarked, that
though individual instances of unfeeling barbarity
might be quoted, yet, as a race, the Esquimaux
display much less of savage ferocity and unrelenting
cruelty than is commonly observed among barbarous
nations. The horrid indifference to the condition
of others, and the desire of appropriation, are the
worst features in their character. The temptation
of a knife, a saw, or any edged tool, is irresistible;
and they often show considerable ingenuity in accom-
plishing their abstractions. They are indolent and
very improvident, and hence the famine from which
they so frequently suffer. They have no vestige of
learning among them, and their gratifications are
altogether sensual. In some points of morality
they are exceedingly deficient, but they show some
traces of a better nature, which we can contemplate
with pleasure. They are in general mild and good-
natured, and the greatest harmony prevails among
them. The women are treated with kindness, and
the affection which subsists between a mother and
her offspring, is, if possible, stronger than what obtains in civilized communities. Her whole attention
is bestowed upon her infant, and the punishment of
a child is altogether unknown. I have frequently,
by way of testing their affection, offered them valuable articles in barter for the rich furs in which
they envelope the children; but I invariably met

with a refusal, unless they had the means of supply-
ing the deficiency at hand. The strictest honesty
is practised among themselves, and this appears the
more wonderful when we consider their propensity
to steal from us; nor can it be explained by the
strength of the temptation alone which our articles
offer, for when any one of their number has obtained
similar articles, the others show no disposition to
steal from him. They are hardy and adventurous,
and well skilled in the various arts of the chase.
In general, the Esquimaux confine their attacks to
the seal and walrus, but in Hogarth's Sound they
kill from six to twelve whales annually. The
method which they adopt for this purpose is highly
ingenious, and similar in principle to that practised
by our fishermen in the South Seas. The harpoon
is formed from the outer layer of the jaw-bone of a
young whale, and the line is composed of the skin
of a particular species of seal. It is attached to the
centre of an apparatus resembling a large sieve, and
formed principally of whalebone. When the whale
is struck, the effect of this contrivance is to retard
its progress through the water, and being rendered
buoyant by the attachment of inflated seal-skins, it
serves to point out the spot where the animal is
rising to the surface to respire. In conducting
their operations against these and other inhabitants
of the Arctic deep, the Esquimaux are obliged to

migrate from place to place, in consequence of the ever-varying condition of the surface of the sea. Besides these necessary migrations, they often undertake long journeys without any very definite purpose. Sometimes the distance of two and even three hundred miles is travelled over in their sledges during winter. They are expert navigators, and the Nugumiuts, or those who dwell to the south of Hogarth's Sound, not unfrequently cross Hudson's Strait in their oomiak, without chart or compass, for the purpose of procuring wood from the natives of the Labrador coast.

After noticing the leading features of the bodily formation and mental constitution of the Esquimaux, we are naturally led to inquire into the cause which has retarded their progress towards civilization. Is it the effect of their physical structure, or can we attribute it to the circumstances by which they are surrounded? If, as is said, the mind of man has a close and intimate connection with his cerebral organization, and deficiency of development marks inferiority of intellect,—then the savage, unaided, cannot advance beyond a state of barbarism, nor will any education, however elaborate, raise him at once to the condition of civilization. Experience and observation both tend to confirm this view of the case ; but, as we find considerable diversity of character among savage nations, we may reasonably expect to find also great difference in their capability of improvement. When reviewing the more prominent features of Eenoolooapik's mind, we discovered a considerable development of those faculties which were best suited to place him in harmony with his condition; and he evinced a great aptitude for acquiring such knowledge as came within the range of those faculties. He also wanted many of the darker traits which are so often found among other savages; and if anything can be inferred from his solitary example, it would lead to the conclusion that though the Esquimaux are incapable of elevating themselves, yet, upon the proper impulse being given, they are susceptible of great improvement.

In addition to the facility of studying the habits of the Esquimaux, our situation enabled us to enjoy the recreation of a walk on shore. On one occasion, accompanied by a friend, I undertook an excursion for some distance into the interior, for the purpose of deer-hunting. We travelled for a few miles along the border of a lake, when, turning the abrupt corner of a hill, we found a broad plain stretching out before us. It was nearly covered with vegetation, and seemed to be an excellent place for our purpose. It was bounded on the farther side by a ridge of hills, which were almost entirely clear of snow, and the country generally had a rather milder appearance than I had been accustomed to see in those regions.

R

We crossed the plain without meeting any game, and thinking that it might be found in the higher ground, we ascended the steep sides of the hills. Here we were equally unsuccessful, but the extensive view which our elevated situation afforded, was some reward for our toil. The naked rock, split into fragments by the frost, everywhere formed the surface, except upon the plain which we had traversed, and a narrow tract along the banks of the lake. The dissolving of the snow had given every depression on the hills the appearance of a river bed, and converted into lakes the numerous cup-shaped valleys with which the surface of the country was diversified. There was but little of that wild sublimity of scenery which most parts of the country present. The feeling of solitude—of complete and utter separation from the world—was what the view produced. It bore no mark of the presence of man—nor did it seem to yield anything which could contribute to his existence. All was hushed and lonely—no sound broke upon the stillness around us—eternal silence seemed to reign over the desolate land.

Fatigued and disappointed, we dragged ourselves over the rough and broken country to the lake along which we had at first journeyed, and on arriving there we were gratified to find a party of our men, who had set out with us in the morning, still pursuing the salmon fishing. Like us they had been unsuccessful—the season being too far advanced for finding salmon in the higher latitudes. Embarking in the boat, we rowed down the lake which opened near the harbour, and were thus saved a long and tedious journey to the ship.

From the rocks forming the shores of the harbour, and adjoining country, I procured specimens of *granite, gneiss, mica slate, porphyry,* and *hornblende.* Notwithstanding the great hardness of some of these rocks, their disintegration is rapidly effected by the freezing of water in their interstices. The amount of change annually produced in the Arctic regions by this cause, aided by the transporting power of running water, must be very great. During the melting of the snow every insignificant valley has its rivulet, and these uniting form large rivers, which, loaded with sediment, pursue their way to the ocean. The quantity of matter brought down in this way is so great at times as to render the sea turbid for a considerable distance from the shore ; and the force and impetuosity of these torrents is such, that not sedimentary matter alone, but even enormous masses of rock, are torn up and swept away. In this way a great collection of heterogeneous materials takes place at their point of junction with the sea, producing a shoal, which, however, extends only for a little distance, as the force of the tides is sufficient, at least in Hogarth's Sound, to remove the lighter matter.

The weather, which as before stated had interfered with our fishing operations, still continued unpropitious, so much so that we now scarcely ever sent out the boats. It was therefore determined on, as a last alternative, that we should proceed to the top of the Sound, in the hope that we would find it less tempestuous there. This plan we were prevented from carrying into execution at the time that it was resolved upon, in consequence of the wind being from the north ; as it was feared that if we left the harbour with a foul wind, in such an unsettled state of the weather, we might be blown off the land altogether. We were therefore constrained to wait until it should change.

On the 18th, the wind coming from the south, we got under weigh with the intention of proceeding up the Sound, but in consequence of the strong tide and other circumstances preventing the ship wearing speedily, we were obliged again to let go the anchor to keep her off the rocks. The anchor caught the ground in time to prevent her striking forcibly at first, but she swung round and went ashore. When the tide left us there were not over four feet water aft, but with the assistance of a couple of warps from the ships still at anchor, we got off the following tide without any damage.

On the morning of the 19th the wind had changed, and we could not move until the 21st, when we once more got under weigh. During the night of that date it again came to blow heavily from the north. Fearing that the ice, driven down by these northerly winds, would hem us in, and concluding that the weather was entirely broken up in consequence of the advanced period of the season, on the 22d we bade farewell to the Sound, and bore up for home, where we arrived in safety on the 11th of October.

CHAPTER VI.

HAVING now concluded our description of the Sound, it only remains for us to inquire whether anything has been elicited which can be rendered available for the purposes of the whale-fishery; or whether any other means than those hitherto followed can be devised for its prosecution, which would render its success more certain.

In discussing these subjects, it will be necessary again to advert to the causes which have brought about the failures already mentioned. These we have stated to be the increased difficulty in reaching the fishing stations, in consequence of the accumulation of ice, and the animals having deserted some of their usual haunts,—these places being, as it is termed, "fished out."

Whether Hogarth's Sound might be easily reached at a sufficiently early period of the year, to insure success, cannot be said to be satisfactorily determined. It will be recollected that it was the latter

end of July before we arrived at its entrance, and
that we then found it blocked up with ice. This
circumstance might perhaps be thought to lead to
the conclusion that it had not been accessible previous to that time; but so rapid are the changes
which take place among the ice, that it is highly
probable that it might have been entered long before
the time we attempted it. The whale-fishing vessels
have frequently penetrated to the west-land about
the latitude of 66° north, during the months of May
and June; and there is every reason to believe that
they would have found it much more easy to gain the
entrance of Hogarth's Sound, than to reach the land
at a more northerly point. But as the attempt has not
yet been made, we will not insist upon its practica-
bility. We may, however, remark, that the obstacles
appear to be much less formidable than those which
obstruct the route to the usual fishing ground.

The second cause of failure noticed, namely, the
places being " fished out," cannot at all apply to this
new station; for, beyond the few which the Esquimaux kill, the fish are entirely undisturbed; and it
is presumed they would at first fall an easy prey to
the fishermen. Indeed, we become convinced of this
when we consider the puny nature of the weapons
with which the Esquimaux kill them. The fact of
their abounding in great numbers in Hogarth's
Sound, would appear to be completely established;

but as it is problematical whether the fishery could be carried on with success in this place, in the usual manner, we will now proceed to inquire whether any means exist by which the difficulties which have hitherto retarded the operations may be avoided.

For this purpose, let us in the first place review what we have discovered concerning the seasons of the year during which the animals are to be found there. Early in September we saw them pouring into the Sound, and we were informed by the Esquimaux that they would not leave it until it became completely frozen up; which, according to the same account, would not be till the month of January. They also stated, that when they undertook long journeys over the ice in spring, when hunting for young seals, they saw whales in great numbers at the edge of the land-floe. From this it would appear that they go no farther away than the frozen surface of the ocean obliges them; and so soon as the ice begins to break up in the Sound, they return to it, and remain there until the heat of summer has entirely wasted away the land-floe. The period at which the ice would allow them to enter would be about the beginning of May; and the complete disruption of the land-floe would take place in July—varying, of course, according to the season. In the intervals, then, between September and January—and between the beginning of May and the end of

July, we should find the whales numerous in the Sound.

During the former of these periods, the fear of being wintered would prevent the ships, as at present provided, from remaining—even if the weather was such that they could fish. Again, during the latter period, it is yet doubtful whether they could enter the Sound in time. It appears, therefore, that the method of conducting the fishery with uniform success would be to provide the ships for wintering, and to send them out at such a time that they might enter the Sound and find a harbour before the winter set in. They might then prosecute the fishery, as soon as the ice permitted them, in spring—return home with their cargoes—and be got out again in time for the following winter. By this plan greater expense would, no doubt, be incurred—the men being kept almost the whole year employed; but there is little doubt that this would be far more than counterbalanced by the increased returns.

Another plan has been proposed, and it is one which appears to be in many respects preferable to that which we have just described. It is at once to establish a settlement at some part which the whales are known to frequent, and to prosecute the fishery whenever the season would permit. Vessels might then be sent out with stores, and to bring home the produce in the proper season. It appears

to me that Hogarth's Sound is remarkably well
adapted for this purpose, as from the southern situation of its entrance there is no fear of its being so
much blocked up with ice, but that communication
could be had with the settlers at some period of the
season. The vessels would also incur much less risk
from the ice in proceeding to a settlement at this,
than at any point farther north.

It is unnecessary to enter into a full detail of the
economy of such an establishment. That will readily
suggest itself to those conversant with such matters.
But we may remark that a number of men, not much
greater than the crew of a whaler, would at first
suffice. They would require to be provided with
comfortable houses—a large stock of provisions—
plenty of fishing gear—and one or two small vessels
in which they might go to some distance from the
settlement for the purpose of fishing, if such should
be found necessary. The chief objects to be attended
to when not carrying on the fishing would be the
comfort and employment of the men. Without ample
provision for, and strict attention to these, the rigours
of the climate could not be borne; while, under
proper management, its severity would be comparatively harmless. This is sufficiently demonstrated
by the health of the crews of the ships employed on
discovery. The Danes also on the east side, and
much farther north than the proposed settlement

would be, enjoy excellent health. Major Fasting, at Leively, of whom I have before spoken, informed me that, so far from being unable to follow his usual avocations during winter, he chose that season for making his journeys among the settlements under his superintendance. The greater facility of making these journeys on the ice, no doubt influenced him in his choice ; but he positively assured me that the intensity of the cold was not such as to prevent him from undertaking them.

During the winter, when fishing could not be carried on, sufficient employment might be found in hunting seals—this being the time when the Esquimaux kill the greatest number of them. In the latter part of summer and beginning of autumn, deer-hunting and salmon-fishing would form most agreeable recreations, and afford an excellent and salutary change of food.

The produce of such a settlement need not consist of oil and whalebone alone. The rich furs with which the animals of that country are covered, would prove valuable commodities. Ermines are found around the shores of the Sound in great numbers. Of this I was not only informed by Eenoolooapik, but I have frequently seen them, and even sometimes caught them. On the shore, after a slight fall of snow, innumerable traces of them are to be observed in every direction.

The Esquimaux, who are a harmless and docile race, and already practically acquainted with the art of whaling, would prove powerful auxiliaries ; while the benefits which would result to themselves from the establishment of settlements among them, are altogether incalculable. On the eastern shore of Davis' Strait, settlements have existed for a considerable time, and missionary efforts have effected a great change in the moral improvement and general comfort of the natives ; while, on the western coast, nothing has as yet been done to reclaim the poor benighted savages from their rude and debasing superstitions. And, indeed, the rigour of the climate is such, and the difficulties and dangers to be encountered so many, that it can scarcely be expected that Christian philanthropy will soon direct attention to that region as a field for missionary enterprise, unless in connection with some such establishment as has just been proposed. Thus, there are motives of a far higher character than the mere accumulation of wealth by commercial speculation, to urge philanthropic and enterprising men to make trial of such a scheme. And surely it must be cheering to every enlightened mind to think, that the moral darkness which overspreads those regions with more deep and dreary gloom than even their own long polar night discloses, is destined to be dispelled by the genial rays of the Sun of Righteousness. Ay, and it is an

honour well worth aspiring after, to share in aiding
the progress of truth over the earth. And who can
tell but Eenoolooapik may contribute towards pre-
paring his countrymen for the reception of the gospel,
for he has now had a proof of their sad degradation,
and can tell them of the land where the Bible is
believed; so that, trifling as his visit to Britain may
appear, it may be the germ whence civilization may
spring and overspread even that dreary wilderness
of snow.

APPENDIX.

APPENDIX.

———

THE following Tables were drawn up from careful observation of the atmospheric pressure, and temperature of the air and sea. The direction and strength of the wind, and state of the weather, were at the same time carefully noted, and are inserted in order that they may be compared with the indications of the Barometer.

For the sake of convenience, figures have been used to express the strength of the wind; and the following is an explanation of these:—0, calm; 1, very light air; 2, light air; 3, light breeze; 4, moderate breeze; 5, smart breeze; 6, fresh breeze; 7, moderate gale; 8, fresh gale; 9, very strong gale; 10, hurricane.

I have considered it unnecessary to give the Latitude and Longitude for each day, as the changes of situation were often very trifling. I have here, however, subjoined a general account of the spaces traversed during each month.

May.—The range over which the observations for this month were made, extended from latitude 58° N. longitude 30° W. to latitude 72° N. longitude 58° W. The ship's course was to the north-west.

June.—The observations for this period were made between latitude 72° N. longitude 58° W. and latitude 75° 10′ N. longitude 60° W. The course of the ship was still to the north-west.

July.—The change of situation during this month extended from latitude 75° 10′ N. longitude 60° W. to latitude 65° N. longitude 63° W. The ship's course was to the south-west.

August.—The observations for this month were made between latitude 64° 10′ N. longitude 63° W. and latitude 66° 20′ N. longitude 68° W. By referring to the Chart of Hogarth's Sound, the situation of the ship during any period of this month may be determined.

September.—Between the 4th and 22d of this month, the ship remained in Parker's Harbour, latitude 65° 9′ N. longitude 65° 30′ W. The few observations noted after leaving this place were made while running across the entrance of Davis' Strait and round Cape Farewell. It will be observed that the temperature of the sea gradually rose as we left the ice ; and it may be remarked that the occasional elevation of the temperature of the sea, registered in these Tables, is to be explained by the ship having been at a considerable distance from any large collection of ice.

METEOROLOGICAL TABLE.

MAY 1840.

Week Day.	Month Day.	ATMOSPHERIC PRESSURE.		TEMPERATURE.		
				Atmosphere.		
		8 A. M.	6 P. M.	8 A. M.	2 P. M.	6 P. M.
Friday........	1	30. 08	30. 04			37
Saturday......	2	30. 06	30. 02			35
Sunday........	3	29. 74	29. 70			36
Monday......	4	29. 65	29. 95			42
Tuesday......	5	30. 15	30. 40	36		36
Wednesday...	6	30. 42	30. 48	56	56	
Thursday.....	7	30. 45	30. 45	36		
Friday........	8	30. 34	30. 30	38	35	34
Saturday......	9	30. 10	30. 00	38	35	34
Sunday........	10	29. 94	30. 00	35	35	35
Monday......	11	29. 86	29. 80	35	34	34
Tuesday......	12	29. 70	29. 60	34	33	33
Wednesday...	13	29. 50	29. 46	31	31	30
Thursday.....	14	29. 50	29. 64	32	33	32
Friday........	15	29. 66	29. 70	30	31	32
Saturday......	16	29. 58	29. 55	32	32	33
Sunday	17	29. 50	29. 60	38	36	32
Monday......	18	29. 50	29. 45	30	31	29
Tuesday......	19	29. 40	29. 60	30	34	32
Wednesday....	20	29. 60	29. 40	32	32	32
Thursday.....	21	29. 50	29. 65	32	34	32
Friday........	22	29. 80	29. 80	31	36	30
Saturday......	23	29. 50	29. 40	36	34	32
Sunday........	24	29. 40	29. 45	24	25	24
Monday.......	25	39. 50	29. 62	29	30	32
Tuesday.......	26	29. 64	29. 70	30	32	28
Wednesday ...	27	29. 70	29. 70	29	30	28
Thursday.....	28	29. 80	29. 80	30	30	29
Friday........	29	29. 78	29. 70	28	29	27
Saturday......	30	29. 70	29. 68	30	32	28
Sunday	31	29. 70	29. 72	28	26	24

METEOROLOGICAL TABLE.

MAY 1840.—(*Continued.*)

Month Day.	WINDS. Direction. A. M.	WINDS. Direction. P. M.	Strength. A.M.	Strength. P.M.	Remarks.	Situation.
1	North	NE by E	3	5	Clear.	At Sea.
2	ENE	ENE	6	6	Cloudy.	
3	East	East	10	10	Hazy. Rain.	Cape Farewell.
4	East	E by S	10	10	Do. Do.	
5	ESE	SE	8	6	Clear.	Entrance Davis' Strait.
6	SW		2	0	Fine Weather.	
7	NNE	NNE	4	3	Cloudy.	Streams of ice.
8	West	NW	3	3	Hazy.	
9	NNE	NE	3	3	Do.	
10	NE		4	0	Do.	Middle of Strait.
11	NE by N	W by N	4	4	Do. Snow.	
12	WSW	W by N	4	6	Do.	
13	South	SSW	6	6	Foggy. Snow.	South-west Pack.
14	SW	SW	5	5	Cloudy.	
15	SSE	SSW	6	6	Foggy. Snow.	
16	SSE	Variable	4	2	Clear.	Wiede Fiord.
17	SSW	NNW	2	4	Clear. Snow.	Reef Coll.
18	NE	NNE	4	8	Cloudy.	Loose ice.
19	East	West	4	3	Clear.	Disco.
20	North		4	0	Do.	Leively.
21	NE	NE	4	4	Dull weather.	Ice.
22	South	SSE	5	4	Cloudy.	Streams of ice.
23	West	WSW	2	4	Hazy. Snow.	South-East Bay.
24	North	NNE	7	6	Snowy.	Waygatz Strait.
25			0	0	Clear.	Four Island Point.
26		ENE	0	6	Beautiful weather	Black Hook.
27	NE	NE	6	6	Clear ; very cold.	Open water.
28	NE	NE	6	6	Clear.	Cape Lawson.
29	NE	NE by N	7	7	Do.	Open water.
30	NE	NE	5	3	Cloudy.	Dark Head.
31	Northerly	NE	1	2	Hoar frost.	Streams of ice.

METEOROLOGICAL TABLE.

June 1840.

Week Day.	Month Day.	ATMOSPHERIC PRESSURE.		TEMPERATURE.			
				Atmosphere.			Sea.
		8 A. M.	6 P. M.	8 A. M.	2 P. M.	6 P. M.	
Monday......	1	29. 80	29. 78	36	34	32	30
Tuesday......	2	29. 70	29. 50	28	27	26	30
Wednesday...	3	29. 34	29. 28	23	24	24	28
Thursday.....	4	29. 30	29. 50	26	28	27	29
Friday.......	5	29. 70	29. 80	28	28	27	30
Saturday.....	6	29. 98	29. 98	32	44	36	30
Sunday......	7	29. 98	30. 20	46	50	44	30
Monday......	8	30. 18	30. 00	48	50	42	32
Tuesday......	9	30. 08	29. 95	44	44	36	32
Wednesday...	10	29. 95	29. 84	42	48	40	32
Thursday.....	11	29. 80	29. 94	42	46	38	32
Friday.......	12	29. 94	29. 84	44	54	40	30
Saturday.....	13	29. 80	29. 83	52	82	40	30
Sunday.......	14	29. 80	29. 78	34	36	32	30
Monday......	15	29. 74	29. 70	30	32	30	30
Tuesday......	16	29. 64	29. 70	34	36	32	30
Wednesday...	17	29. 65	29. 60	48	48	33	30
Thursday.....	18	29. 72	29. 70	54	58	45	31
Friday.......	19	29. 60	29. 60	33	34	33	32
Saturday.....	20	29. 50	29. 48	40	50	32	30
Sunday......	21	29. 52	29. 57	34	44	34	30
Monday......	22	29. 48	29. 18	42	46	36	29
Tuesday......	23	29. 13	29. 29	34	37	33	29
Wednesday...	24	29. 40	29. 50	40	44	32	30
Thursday.....	25	29. 52	29. 53	49	60	32	30
Friday.......	26	29. 35	29. 45	42	33	31	30
Saturday.....	27	29. 55	29. 62	43	56	37	29
Sunday.......	28	29. 59	29. 52	48	37	31	30
Monday......	29	29. 45	29. 10	32	29	30	29
Tuesday......	30	28. 70	29. 30	33	40	36	29½

METEOROLOGICAL TABLE.

June 1840.—(*Continued.*)

Month Day.	WINDS.				Remarks.	Situation.
	Direction.		Strength.			
	A. M.	P. M.	A.M.	P.M.		
1		Northerly	0	2	Cloudy.	Frow Islands.
2	ENE	NE	4	6	Hazy.	Streams of ice.
3	NE	E by N	4	4	Strong hoar frost.	Frow Islands.
4	NE	WSW	2	4	Hazy.	Do.
5	WNW	SW	4	2	Fog. Snow.	Do.
6	SE	ESE	3	2	Very clear.	Loose ice.
7		WSW	0	4	Fine weather.	Berry Island.
8	ESE	ESE	2	4	Clear.	Ice.
9	SW	SW	4	8	Thick snow.	Close beset.
10	SW	SW	7	6	Hazy. Rain.	Near Baffin Isles.
11	SW	SSE	5	4	Clear.	Close beset.
12	SW		1	0	Clear.	Do.
13		Westerly	0	2	Very fine weather.	Do.
14	ENE	NE	4	7	Thick fog.	Sugarloaf Point.
15	ENE	NE by E	5	4	Foggy.	Baffin Isles.
16	NE	ESE	3	3	Hazy. Snow.	Melville Bay.
17	SW	NW	2	2	Do. Do.	Large floes.
18				0	0	Fine weather.	Do.
19	South	SW	3	6	Fog. Snow.	Devil's Thumb.
20	South	SW	2	4	Hazy. Rain.	Land floe.
21		WSW	0	2	Do. Do.	Do.
22	Variable	WSW	1	8	Do. Do.	Do.
23	SW by W	WSW	9	6	Hazy. Snow.	Hecla wrecked.
24	WSW	WSW	4	2	Fog. Snow.	Land floe.
25		ENE	0	3	Fine weather.	Do.
26	ENE	SW	2	5	Snow. Clear.	Do.
27	SW		3	0	Hazy.	Do.
28	NE	NNE	3	5	Hazy. Snow.	Do.
29	NE	NE by E	6	8	Cloudy. Snow.	Do.
30	SW	SSW	9	4	Hazy.	Cape Walker.

METEOROLOGICAL TABLE.

JULY 1840.

| Week Day. | Month Day. | ATMOSPHERIC PRESSURE. | | TEMPERATURE. | | | |
| | | | | Atmosphere. | | | Sea. |
		8 A. M.	6 P. M.	8 A. M.	2 P. M.	6 P. M.	
Wednesday...	1	29. 58	29. 68	48	64	29	29
Thursday.....	2	29.90	29. 91	42	62	27½	29
Friday	3	29. 70	29. 75	34	40	29	29
Saturday	4	29. 82	29. 86	40	50	32	29¾
Sunday	5	29. 94	30. 10	44	49	31	29½
Monday......	6	30. 12	30. 15	37	60	35	29½
Tuesday......	7	30. 00	30. 02	37	45	30	32
Wednesday ...	8	29. 96	29. 98	31	70	27	32
Thursday.....	9	30. 02	29. 99	36	45	34	31½
Friday	10	29. 98	29. 99	37	60	30	31
Saturday.....	11	30. 00	29. 95	35	78	38⅔	32
Sunday	12	29. 65	39. 54	44	80	48	32½
Monday......	13	29. 60	29. 65	48	62	39	34
Tuesday.....	14	29. 66	29 69	52	58	39	35
Wednesday...	15	29. 69	29. 68	39	42	40	36
Thursday.....	16	29. 50	29. 60	40	54	36	36
Friday........	17	29. 70	29. 80	32	44	40	36
Saturday......	18	29. 73	29. 70	39	42	31	35
Sunday......	19	29. 70	29. 68	35	50	34	34
Monday.......	20	29. 68	29. 68	37	45	37	35½
Tuesday......	21	29. 40	29. 33	39	38	36	36
Wednesday ...	22	29. 33	29. 55	45	52	37	36
Thursday ...	23	29. 50	29. 51	36	38	36	32½
Friday........	24	29. 38	29. 36	37	43	33	32
Saturday......	25	29. 36	29. 34	33	53	31	32
Sunday......	26	29. 36	29. 30	32	50	33	33
Monday.......	27	29. 40	29. 42	38	42	31	34
Tuesday......	28	29. 46	29. 44	39	40	32	35
Wednesday...	29	29. 30	29. 32	32	36	34	36
Thursday.....	30	29. 26	29. 33	35	40	34	33
Friday........	31	29. 36	29. 30	35	38	32	33

METEOROLOGICAL TABLE.

July 1840.—(*Continued.*)

Month Day.	WINDS.		Strength.		Remarks.	Situation.
	Direction.					
	A. M.	P. M.	A.M.	P.M.		
1			0	0	Beautiful weather	Cape Walker.
2	North	NE	2	2	Fog.	Close beset.
3	NNE	NE	2	3	Hoar frost.	Do.
4	Westerly	Westerly	2	2	Foggy.	Do.
5	Variable		2	0	Do.	Do.
6		Westerly	0	3	Clear.	Do.
7	NNE	NE by N	2	3	Thick fog.	Do.
8	WSW	NNE	1	1	Clear generally.	Do.
9	North	NNE	1	2	Clear.	Do.
10	NE by N	East	3	2	Fine weather.	Do.
11		ENE	0	4	Do.	Ice open southward.
12	ENE	SW by W	4	5	Do.	Devil's Thumb.
13	South	West	4	2	Do.	Wilcox Point.
14	NNE	NNE	4	6	Do.	Sugarloaf Point.
15	East	ESE	4	5	Do.	Saunderson's Hope.
16	ENE	SSE	5	3	Do.	Disco.
17	WNW	WSW	5	2	Fog. Rain.	Middle of Strait.
18	NNE	North	3	2	Thick fog.	Edge of Pack.
19	SW	South	4	5	Fog. Rain.	Do.
20	Calm	SE	0	3	Hazy. Rain.	Do.
21	South	SSE	4	7	Thick fog. Rain.	Do.
22			0	0	Fog.	Do.
23	SSW	SE	2	3	Do.	Do.
24	ENE	ENE	3	6	Do. Rain.	Do.
25	NW	SSE	3	7	Thick fog.	Cape Walsingham.
26	ENE	WNW	2	4	Do.	Loose ice.
27	SW	ENE	4	7	Thick fog gearly.	Saunderson's Tower.
28	ENE	SE	4	4	Fog. Snow.	Cruizing off Sound.
29	ENE	ENE	4	5	Sleet. Snow.	Do.
30	ENE	BNE	4	3	Hazy.	Do.
31	SSE	SE	2	8	Hazy.	Do.

METEOROLOGICAL TABLE.

August 1840.

Week Day.	Month Day.	ATMOSPHERIC PRESSURE.		TEMPERATURE.			
				Atmosphere.			Sea.
		8 A. M.	6 P. M.	8 A. M.	2 P. M.	6 P. M.	
Saturday....	1	29.20	29.15	33	36	35	34½
Sunday......	2	29.30	29.60	36	37	36	35
Monday......	3	29.60	29.75	35	43	32	34
Tuesday......	4	29.79	29.82	42	78	50	33½
Wednesday..	5	29.80	29.79	36	46	32	31
Thursday....	6	29.79	29.85	50	44	36	29
Friday	7	29.80	29.80	40	56	33	29½
Saturday	8	29.55	29.48	46	64	33	28
Sunday......	9	29.50	29.60	37	54	38	29
Monday......	10	29.70	29.80	40	62	38	29
Tuesday.....	11	29.80	29.82	37	52	44	33
Wednesday..	12	29.80	29.80	36	64	37	35
Thursday....	13	29.80	29.85	49	56	44	36
Friday	14	29.86	29.85	39	56	39	39
Saturday	15	29.85	29.88.	48	78	43	40
Sunday......	16	29.90	29.90	45	43	40	40
Monday.....	17	29.92	29.96	46	60	40	42
Tuesday......	18	29.84	29.64	40	40	39	40
Wednesday..	19	29.46	29.46	39	40	36	38
Thursday....	20	29.46	29.20	39	40	33	36
Friday.......	21	28.98	29.04	37	38	37	35
Saturday	22	29.06	29.08	35	47	40	34½
Sunday......	23	29.06	29.16	38	42	37	35
Monday.....	24	29.29	29.39	43	50	39	35
Tuesday......	25	29.32	29.39	40	47	37	35½
Wednesday..	26	29.56	29.70	41	49	43	36
Thursday....	27	29.76	29.78	40	41	39	36½
Friday......	28	29.46	29.40	39	40	36	34
Saturday	29	29.50	29.60	40	42	35	32
Sunday......	30	29.76	30.00	46	48	36	30
Monday.....	31	30.00	29.95	40	39	34	33½

METEOROLOGICAL TABLE.

August 1840.—(*Continued.*)

Month Day.	WINDS.				Remarks.	Situation.
	Direction.		Strength.			
	A. M.	P. M.	A.M.	P.M.		
1	SSW	E by S	6	5	Foggy. Rain.	Saunderson's Tower.
2	NE	West	5	3	Hazy. Rain.	Ent. of Hogarth's Sound.
3	NW	NE	4	3	Clear.	Among loose ice.
4	Variable	Variable	1	1	Fine Weather.	Do.
5	ENE	SSE	5	4	Do.	Do.
6	NNW	North	2	1	Clear generally.	Packed ice.
7	Westerly	Westerly	2	2	Fine Weather.	Do.
8		WSW	0	4	Do.	Do.
9	North	South	4	3	Cloudy.	Do.
10	NNW	SSW	2	4	Beautiful weather	Queen's Cape.
11	SW	SW	5	4	Do.	Open water.
12	Variable	SW	2	4	Do.	Streams of ice.
13	ENE	ENE	1	2	Do.	Bon Accord Harbour.
14	SW	SW	2	2	Do.	Do.
15	SSW	SSW	2	4	Do.	Hogarth's Sound.
16	SSW	SSW	4	4	Fog.	Straggling ice.
17	Variable	Variable	2	2	Thick Fog.	Open water.
18	SSW	SW	5	8	Cloudy.	Do.
19	SSW	SE	8	6	Do.	Do.
20	SSW	SSW	5	5	Hazy.	Keimooksook.
21	SSW	WNW	7	6	Foggy. Rain.	Open water.
22	SSW	WNW	4	5	Do.	Streams of ice.
23	WNW	WNW	5	5	Hazy. Rain.	Do.
24	WNW	Variable	4	2	Clear.	Do.
25	SW	Variable	6	2	Cloudy.	Entrance of Sound.
26	NNE	North	3	4	Fine weather.	Streams of ice.
27	NE	Variable	3	1	Cloudy.	Do.
28	Variable	NNE	1	7	Do.	Do.
29	NNW	NNW	8	8	Clear. Squally.	Edge of pack.
30	NNE	NNW	8	8	Clear.	Do.
31	NNE	NNE	4	6	Do.	Couldrey's Isle.

METEOROLOGICAL TABLE.

September 1840.

Week Day.	Month Day.	ATMOSPHERIC PRESSURE.		TEMPERATURE.			
				Atmosphere.			Sea.
		8 A. M.	6 P. M.	8 A. M.	2 P. M.	6 P. M.	
Tuesday.......	1	29.75	29.62	40	70	35	36½
Wednesday...	2	29.45	29.40	37	40	34	35
Thursday.....	3	29.40	29.52	42	44	36	36
Friday	4	29.40	29.29	38	36	32	36
Saturday......	5	29.30	29.53	38	40	33½	34
Sunday	6	29.63	29.75	39	44	36	33
Monday.......	7	29.75	29.70	40	48	35	34
Tuesday......	8	29.62	29.70	37	46	37	34
Wednesday...	9	29.75	29.75	34	40	33	32½
Thursday.....	10	29.70	29.65	35	40	32	34
Friday........	11	29.44	29.32	33	35	32	33
Saturday......	12	29.45	29.30	34	36	31	32
Sunday	13	29.25	29.25	30	31	30	32
Monday	14	29.65	29.90	34	34	30	31
Tuesday......	15	29.64	29.60	30	33	35	32
Wednesday....	16	29.64	29.68	36	38	34	34
Thursday.....	17	29.35	29.25	30	40	28	31
Friday........	18	28.86	28.80	28	38	30	29
Saturday......	19	29.20	29.18	31	47	32	30
Sunday	20	29.18	29.21	31	34	29	29
Monday.......	21	29.27	29.10	28	29	29	29¼
Tuesday.......	22	29.55	29.56	30	33	32	29
Wednesday...	23	29.29	29.40	31	34	33	30
Thursday.....	24	29.60	29.60	32	36	34	36
Friday	25	29.40	29.45	33	40	36	36
Saturday......	26	29.50	29.55	37	48	38	45
Sunday.......	27	29.60	29.60	40	50	46	50
Monday.......	28	29.62	29.64	50	47	44	49
Tuesday......	29	29.65	29.65	46	52	48	49
Wednesday...	30	29.70	30.00	48	59	44	50

METEOROLOGICAL TABLE.

SEPTEMBER 1840.—(*Continued.*)

Month Day.	WINDS. Direction. A. M.	WINDS. Direction. P. M.	Strength. A.M.	Strength. P.M.	Remarks.	Situation.
1	West	SSW	3	4	Fine Weather.	Entrance of Sound.
2	NNE	NNE	7	7	Cloudy.	Keimooksook.
3	North	North	8	4	Clear.	Mid Channel.
4	SE	SE	8	8	Fog. Snow.	Parker's Harbour.
5	SE	South	5	6	Snow.	Do.
6	SW	Variable	3	2	Hazy.	
7	NNE	NNE	4	6	Clear.	
8	Variable	Westerly	2	3	Do.	
9	NE	NE	4	4	Do.	
10	SE	SE	5	6	Cloudy.	
11	South	ENE	8	4	Fog. Snow.	
12	NE	NE	8	8	Clear.	
13	SE	NE	9	10	Fog. Snow.'	
14	ENE	ENE	7	8	Squally.	
15	ENE	NE	8	3	Cloudy.	
16	NE	SE	7	2	Clear.	
17	SSE	SSE	4	6	Do.	
18	Variable	N by E	3	10	Hazy.	
19	North	West	6	2	Clear.	
20	NW	N by E	3	8	Snow.	
21	NNE	N by E	8	8	Do.	Cape Enderby.
22	NE	North	6	7	Cloudy.	Ice.
23	North	North	8	7	Snow.	At Sea.
24	North	NNW	6	6	Cloudy.	
25	NW	NW	4	4	Fog. Rain.	
26	NW	NE	5	3	Cloudy.	
27	SSW	WNW	5	5	Hazy.	
28	NW	NNW	7	7	Cloudy.	
29	North	NW	6	7	Do.	
30	WNW	NW	7	7	Hazy.	

Lightning Source UK Ltd.
Milton Keynes UK
UKHW011855150821
388662UK00008B/122